Psychoanalysis &
A Historical Story of
GHENGHIS KHAN

Psychoanalysis &
A Historical Story of
GHENGHIS KHAN

Anil Pundlik Gokhale

authorHOUSE®

AuthorHouse™ UK
1663 Liberty Drive
Bloomington, IN 47403 USA
www.authorhouse.co.uk
Phone: 0800.197.4150

Published by AuthorHouse 06/02/2015

ISBN: 978-1-5049-3983-6 (sc)
ISBN: 978-1-5049-3984-3 (e)

Print information available on the last page.

Any people depicted in stock imagery provided by Thinkstock are models,
and such images are being used for illustrative purposes only.
Certain stock imagery © Thinkstock.

This book is printed on acid-free paper.

Because of the dynamic nature of the Internet, any web addresses or links contained in
this book may have changed since publication and may no longer be valid. The views
expressed in this work are solely those of the author and do not necessarily reflect the
views of the publisher, and the publisher hereby disclaims any responsibility for them.

DEDICATION

This book is dedicated to Fighting Spirit and Courage of my Life partner Ms Vasanti.

CONTENTS

WHAT IS THE BOOK ABOUT

This Book is about Political Nightmares of Hate Philosophers, Totalitarian Lesser Gods. The Satire attempts to enter into Navels of 'Political' in the Unconscious. Sigmund Freud's Dream Book has opened marvels beyond imagination for Sciences & Creative Arts. Marxism as the Modern Science is the biggest beneficiary of Freud's discoveries and his method of Interpretation of Fetishism and Illusions. It has provided Marxist historians' means to understand the social, economic and cultural conflicts in Human Minds & Human History in their fullest depths.

In Revision of Dream theory, Nightmares and Anxiety Dreams, are products or caused by traumatic neurosis, Freud concludes that they do not contradict his Dream theory of wish-fulfillment, it only represents Failure of Dream work. Infantile, imperishable traumatic experiences resurface with such a force that it leads to disturbance of sleep.

The modification- attempt for wish fulfillment in these recurrent dreams, has opened up new marvels for interpretation beyond Unconscious. This Book attempts to traverse beyond it through Presentation of Satires based on reincarnation of Legend of GENGHIS KHAN in modern forms of totalitarian political forms of Rule under Capitalism in Crisis. Failure of Dream Work and not the dream theory remains time tested.

GENGHIS KHAN's Satire presented here is conceived as Nightmare of Original Dictator, the greatest, in history, ruthless, Expansionist-Imperialist. His Anxiety Dream of Blood on ICE compels him to invade TANGUT- China for desire of its Princes. Bujt what follws is not wish fulfillment but a trauma. Similarly, I stumbled against Anxiety dream in poetic creations- MAGNUM OPUS - KAMALA of V.D. Savarkar in ANDAMAN Jails under British Ruled Indian subcontinent. The concluding line "The Royal Beds are set on fire and Dreams turn into truth" shaped his philosophy of Rage and Violence. The poetic journey finally result into failure of dream-work I It denotes sexual origins of Philosophy of Hatred! (Verses 871 to 882)". The great cartoonist Sir David Low's "Adolf Hitler- "NIGHTMARE WAITING LIST" (1938) or his Dreamland faces the Situation' makes the same point. It drove me into the heart of the subject of interpreting the Nightmares of propagators of Hate!"

The Book is focused on this limited but most promising area, the dreadful Political Phantasies. The Dictators have attempted to shape the Human history in forms which they felt conducive to satisfy their deeply repressed Oedipal desires. The Dark hours of Night provided them the perfect historical situations and opportunities when the ever alert oedipal fire generates brutal conflict and engulfs the consciousness with disastrous fire. The resultant- disturbance of Sleep and awakening! Interpretation leads to insights into interiors of their mind and History. Object of this Book is to uncover the unfolding historical processes as reflected in the brains of these Super-gods in the in inverted and fetishised forms. What Karl Marx sees in unfolding of History in the external forms, Sigmund Freud sees the same in Dreams. Interpretation of Ten Images of the Satire are Timeless and 'A- Historical' as they constrict and compound events, actors, players and situations in a single unfolding plot. They obey all laws of dream formation- representations, distortion, condensation, superimposition, condescension and symbolism in the interiors of the minds of Dictators. My Genghis Khan totalizes the upheavals of the regimented masses in regression mode and directs their anger towards annihilation of enemy- the 'OTHER'.

Dictators are born as product of history and execute the historical compulsions dictated by Ruling Classes. In modern Epoch of Civilization. GENGHIS KHAN Legend is reborn in ever age to spread the darkness through massive repression, But ALAS, the Dream ends in disaster. Dictators fall amidst the popular awakening and surge for liberation. The destructive blind Oedipal desires meet their limitations. Liberation of mankind lies in redemption from Oedipal Curse and achieving Self Control. It amounts to victory of Joint Venture between Psychoanalysis and Marxism!

PREFACE

This is my second tryst with AUTHORHOUSE is continuation of my exploration of Socio Political Applications in History. The relationship between Psychoanalysis & Marxism, more specifically applications of Psychoanalytic techniques and methods for interpretation of life of modern Dictators and their sudden rise as offshoot of ultra rightwing, movements in History. Amongst Marxist Historians I was inspired by Historian Carl Schorske and his treatment of psychoanalysis and Sigmund Freud. His theoretical discovery that Sigmund Freud's 'Dream Book' is essentially 'counter political' & that Freudian dialectic revolves around fundamental **primal conflict in the mental life of Human being—Father- Son conflict or Repression and Instincts**. The theme is adequately appropriate to be utilized as Universal and General Application for deciphering the historical characteristics of conflicts manifesting in socio political life of individuals, groups, classes, nations and states.

The theme of this Book is Dictators, the Psychopaths, amidst mass movements and role of Psychoanalysis. Dictators not only express their own sickness, mental disorders and primal lusts, but actively evoke mental disorders of masses through collective identification and concealed in the forms of hatred of 'Other' and Ultra nationalism. Psychoanalysis claims to be a Science which can interpret the symbols and symptoms expressed and rooted in the regressive mental disorders and get to the bottom of the conflicts. Interpretative strength becomes mighty force in if integrated with historical science of Marxism. Paul Ricouer's Essays demonstrates their kinship and conversion, in comprehending Historicity and unveiling of 'Fetishism'!

This Mini Book includes four Essays on the same subject. They are namely, Savarkar – A Poetic Genius Or A Philosopher of Rage?, 'Political Psychology of Annajees, 'Devid Low's Legacy and Sigmund Freud & 'A- Historical Storey of Genghis Khan' are applications of Interpretation of Political Psychology of Dictators and value of psychoanalytical discoveries. The first three articles are reproduced, with minor modifications, to those published in Countercurrents.org on 31st December 2010, 5th March 2012 & 7th August 2013 respectively While the fourth is political corollary of Freud's Auxiliary theory – Anxiety Dreams or Nightmares!

Article Four- Political psychology of Annajees is interpretative commentary on character and Psychological Anotomy of Modern Gandhian Celibacy Anna Hazare, who led and directed the popular wrath of Anti Corruption movement in 2010, which finally deceased eclipsed the political liberalism of Manmohan Singh Govt. The Celibacy could intelligently fuse his hatred of Female sexuality with Anti- corruption and generated the pathologically obsessive *fantasy of all inclusive repressive Anti Corruption Strong Lokpal Institute casted in the image* of his own psychic repressive agency.

Article Three-Savarkar, Political Genius or a Philosopher of Rage is Response to Ashok Malik's 'Savarkar the man who saw tomorrow' which attempted to prop up the LEGACY of a man who founded Ultra Rightwing Anti- Islamist movement, divergent to Anti Imperialist movement in India. A brilliant Poet and a Freedom fighter, who buckled under British Prison's hardships and succumbed to creation of Indian version of Fascist ideology. The Article traces this transformation In the analysis of Savarkar's poetic creations during ANDAMAN IMPRISOINMENT. It discovers genesis of a movement which finally threatened the democratic and political liberalism of modern India.

Article Two - Sir David Low's heroic cartoonish brings forth its value as Critical Tool against repression and muzzling. His Incessant cartoonish triad against Fascism Dictators & Adolf Hitler has earned him a Unique place in History and in Arts & Literature. My essay discovers similarity and kinship between Freudian Psychoanalysis and Cartoonish of David Low, both born in navels of Unconscious, as response to dreams, dreaming as working-material and as shaped by critical rational intellectual capacities dispersing the clouds of repression. Both developed identical methodologies of enquiry, investigation, into representations and interpretation of Imagery. I have identified the method as dialectical and historical in classical sense. Legacy of Sir David Low- who aroused sense of Humor and not Sense of Horror (Christopher Andreae)

Article One, Genghis Khan's NIGHTMARE, picks up the most significant stumbling block, and difficulty Sigmund Freud faced against his 'Wish Fulfillment' theory of dreams. In the wake of World War I and its aftermath, Freud and associates came across number of cases of Traumatic & War Neurosis. Sigmund Freud confronted the difficulties in Interpretation of recurrent Anxiety Dreams and nightmares of people "who have experienced a shock, or severe trauma'. He admits that they rere "regularly taken back in their dreams into the traumatic situation".. Further he says, *"According to our hypotheses about the function of dreams this should not occur. What wishful impulse could be satisfied by harking back in this way to this exceedingly distressing traumatic experience? It is hard to guess "*. What ends up the dreams of this kind are "forcing to the surface the material of distressing events". One gives up sleep from dread of the failure of the function of dreaming

Freud kept on revisiting the dilemma and revised and refashioned his theory to interpret the Nightmares as expressing "failure of functions of Dream work". Psychoanalysis, like an archeologist penetrates into deeper layers of unconscious to discover dream as 'fulfillment of a wish dating back to earliest childhood". Sigmund Freud regarded this point as the 'Naval Point' beyond which it is impossible to understand the meaning concealed within". Freud had first spelt out that "the seemingly nonsensical connections and displacements of ideas, and the regressive, hallucinatory nature of the dream thoughts which nevertheless awaken consciousness and are experienced as if they were real during the dream".

Again in Interpretation of Dreams' he had partially attempted to interpret dream of patient- Anxiety Dream, 'Father, don't you see I'm burning?' where in the distressing desire ends up with generation of high level of anxiety. In Project for Scientific Psychology as early as 1889- says- the seemingly nonsensical connections and displacements of ideas, and the **regressive, hallucinatory nature of the dream thoughts** which nevertheless awaken consciousness and are experienced as if they were real during the dream. This is the po0int which Freud makes- in failure of **Dream Work sponsored under the edges of repression, censoring agency fails to carry out the functions** of displacement, condensation and other forms of representation of the ideas. The regression to primal and infantile wishes hallucinate as imagery of phantoms and monsters, as forces playing havocs in modern civilized society.

Reading Thomas Swan's imaginative piece on Genghis Khan fired my imagination to write this storey. Portraying him as the first Modern dictator who unleashed and awakened the forms of annihilation of enemies unparalleled in History all over Europe, Asia and the Muslim world, I thought *brought me close to understand Freud's Interpretation of Nightmares*. The satire traces the recurrence of phenomena in different forms of and stages of Civilization till twenty First Century. The modern occurrence is Capitalism and the economies in modern forms. It coincides with the Paleontologist view of Evolution. The first event, GHENGHIS Nightmare or Anxiety Dream is *'Red blood on White Ice' can be interpreted as hallucination imagery of castration?* By His life storey resurrects as recurring dream of a Dictator who suffered from War Neurosis and his life ended at the hands of Princess of Tangut (Central China). All successive dictators of modern times under Capitalism had the same fate. Each of them have assumed the role of Patriotic and ruthless Unifiers of Nations. Fascism & Nazism are the recurrent dreams of such Dictators and the NIGHTMARE is destined to fail but will continue to repeat itself till self realization is achieved and Oedipus Complex is conquered.

The Article is unfolding of the Phantasy in Modern times- a Satire A *–Historical; Storey of Genghis Khan, Genghis Khan's recurrent NIGHTMARE* and braces on to quotes from Hindu scriptures, Bhagwat Geeta, part of Hindu Epic Mahabharata-*'paritranaya sadhunam, vinasaya ca duskrtam* **Ddharma-samsthapanarthaya sambhavami** *yuge' yuge* (In order to deliver the pious and to annihilate the miscreants, as well as to reestablish the principles of religion, I advent Myself millennium after millennium). The Ten Screen Shots are quick unfolding of NIGHTMARE which ends with hope of Human Liberation from repression & Slavery

ARTICLE I

A HISTORICAL STORY OF GENGIZ KHAN

Rise & Fall of Dictators
A Political Nightmare Dream and fiction in Making
In order to deliver the pious and to annihilate the
miscreants, as well as to reestablish the principles of
religion, I advent Myself millennium after millennium.

DHARMASANSTHAPNAY SAMBHAVAMI YUGE YUGE

The relation of phantasy to time is in general very important. We may say that it hovers, as it ware, between three times—the three moments of time which our ideation involves. Mental work (Dream Work) is linked to some current impression, some provoking occasion in the present which has been able to arouse one of the subject's major wishes. From here it harks back to a memory of an earlier experience (usually an infantile one) in which this wish was fulfilled; and now it creates a situation relating to the future which represents the fulfillment of the wish. ...which carries about it traces of its origin from the occasion which provoked it and from the memory. Thus, past, present and future are strung together, as it were, on the thread of the wish that runs through them- Henry Miller.

"While the sleeper is obliged to dream, because the relaxation of repression at night allows the upward pressure of the traumatic

1

fixation to become active, there is a failure in the functioning of his dream-work, which would like to transform the memory-traces of the traumatic event into the fulfilment of a wish. In these circumstances it will happen that one cannot sleep, that one gives up sleep from dread of the failure of the function of dreaming."
(Sigmund Freud-Beyond the Pleasure Principle)

Dictators have been regarded not only as cruel but as nightmarish dreamers since they have brought into existence most Inhuman in mankind. All dictators have identical *modes operands* and dreams of all of them have brought into play historical forces of destruction. Hence their anxiety dreams are **A-Historical** in nature. Genghis Khan was one such legendry dreamer whose final dream 'Red Blood on White Snow' interpreted by Oracle stimulated him to undertake final military assault on TANGUT of Central China and which ended up as his Nightmare. 'Red Blood' dream seems to have been triggered by Sexual Desire to capture the most beautiful Princess of TANGUT. Stung by the furious rage and crushing, cruel treatment of the invader Genghis Khan the PRINCESS is said to have retaliated in the Night hours of his Military guarded palace. Princess, avenged the bloodshed **by castrating him** by taking out small knife hidden under her clothes to stop the Cruel Invader from raping her. This storey passed down by Mongol tribesman (told in the book 'In the footsteps of Genghis Khan') **becomes legendry storey of Horror End of every Dictator and provides us** perfect material for interpreting or rather illustrating the Rules of **Anxiety Dream** summarized above by the Psychoanalyst Sigmund Freud.

GHENGHIS KHAN's Life storey is marked by series of invasions, occupations and massacres (He believed to have been sent by God- ("I am the punishment of God...If you had not committed great sins, God would not have sent a punishment like me upon you.") of population, unending and unflinching rage emanating from his **'A-Historical' Unconscious** driven by desire for "**UNIFICATION OF NATION**" ends up on disastrous note. GENGHIS KHAN was reborn in the storey of ADOLF HITELER whose passions had Horrific end in invaded BATTLE GROUND of LENINGRAD. In this fiction- Storey of GENGHIS KHAN whose dream of destruction of INDUS VALLEY remained unfinished on the borders of Delhi Sultanate. GENGHIS is reborn to execute remains of his Horror Dream and falls prey to curse by TANGUT PRINCESS. The **blue Lotus flower** has been steeped in symbolism since the time of the Egyptians and so dear to Genghis Khan is represented in this story **as Dream metaphor for Re-Birth, his flowering sexual desires and Blossoming of empire. The dream was put to an disastrous end by the Princess by castrating the Dictator and herself embracing the death!**

GENGHIS KHAN, Temüjin, was the third-oldest son of his father Yesügei and oldest son of his second wife Hoelun. Legend's storey begins every time, with the hunting excursion, when in a feat of anger, 14-year-old Temüjin killed his half-brother Behter during a fight over hunting spoils. The incident played crucial role in his formation and paved his way to crown him as Head of Tribe. Psychoanalyst can suspect and fathom the sexual dimension – **presence of Oedipus or Castration Complex** beneath this rage which only manifested in his Dream of **'RED BLOOD ON WHITE SNOW'** at latter stage. The Dream storey of GENGHIS KHAN, the EMBRIYO OF **'GREAT DICTATORS' is driven by traumatic fixations and unfolds in this Political Fiction, a Dream Play or a Screen play of Nightmare into another catastrophe.**

In modern times, under capitalism and socio political filth and conditions of chaos and crisis, the storey of GHENGHIS KHAN acquires modern forms, for leading the historical process of mass destructions, genocides, forced labor, annihilation of trade unions and democratic institutions. Such situations are the finest opportunity for the ruling classes, **BULLS, BEARS & BATS** to take charge, create or support the stooge, leader or group of leaders who can ensure the establishment of ruthless Hegemony of Ruling Classes over the amorphous mass of people. The LEADER is turned into 'SAVIOR OF NATION"-BORN to salvage the sinking world ensuring un-hindered attainment of accumulation of wealth and profiteering interests. The dreams of this SAVIOR are made of deep rooted psychical disorders and diseases, complexes and myths nurtured from their child hood and childhood of nations.

Rage triggered by the Fixations is the elemental driving force in execution of these myths, dreams, obsessions and complexes. In modern times and are couched in **Patriotic forms and symbols of NATIONALISM.** Super patriotism needs blossoming of the superego, an internal symbol of the strong father figure: one who would discipline the misbehavior of unruly people. In modern times, GENGHIS the Dictator, works tirelessly to execute the wishes of the BULLS, which stimulate **'Revelation of his 'FATHER EGO' or 'SUPEREGO' in executing punishment** to 'miscreants' through the repressive measures and methods, by instigating genocides and mass annihilation, imprisonments, ethnic massacres, forced labor and concentration camps and Chamber gas for millions. This dream invariably ends in waging horrendous **wars against other NATIONS and G**eographical conquests and finally the disastrous defeats! Today in this fiction, the fearful dream is reignited as fire in the Indus Valley and make alive the Images of Europe under NAZI seize under storm troopers. The Dreams of this Dictator are not New, it was unfinished dream of Genghis Khan.

In modern times, GHENGHIS storey is founded upon the mass regression to archaic. The rage harbored is once against directed against the **HALF BROTHERS, the imagined Rulers and conquers of INDUS VALLEY** of the **TWELFTH CENTURY! This regression can be understood with the ideas and conceptions of Paleontologist Jean-Baptist Lamarck** (1744-1829) who could discover that the most advanced forms of life on this earth still retain the earliest phases of its forms- the **embryo. Psychoanalytic literature can re-invent this Embryo, as Depository of 'Oedipus or castration Complex' at the root of the Anxiety Dream re-activated as rage**. The suppressed instincts alerted rebel and begin their assault on the **foundations of 'Delhi Sultanate**, are represented in this **Horror Dream by the HATRED Brigades OF Demons and Manimals.** GENGHIS KHAN's dream is cyclical in nature and has same end- collapse of his Dictatorship! Each time it begins from its Origins and hence has become-AHISTORICAL in character.

The **Ten SCREEN SHOTS or slides presented below** are the **Paleontological and Psychoanalyst version** of GENGHIS KHAN Dream, unfolding as contemporary-current scenario **in INDUS VALLEY**, a Fiction with a sequence, retrospection in to the past and the fearful fate, future, of attempted fulfillment of these unsatisfied desires. Returning to Henri Miller, we can see that the MENTAL WORK or Dream work, creates images and situations of complex nature from the memory traces by defying the logic. The sequence of images created by dream work, the processes by which the unconscious mind transforms the latent content of the dream into manifest content by using techniques such as Distortion, displacement, compression to disguise or conceal their real meaning from the dreamer. They are aimed at satisfaction of the infantile dream wishes without disturbing sleep. Only logical relation used by dreams is 'just as' or similarity or metaphors. In this Play, the Horror Dream, the **A- Historical Tyrant-the Embryo of Right Wing fascist Dictators** and his Brigades – the activated fixations carry forward the destructive rampage. Sequence and situations, relating to the future, **establishes the Dream rule- Failure in functioning of Dream Work!**

SCENE -1

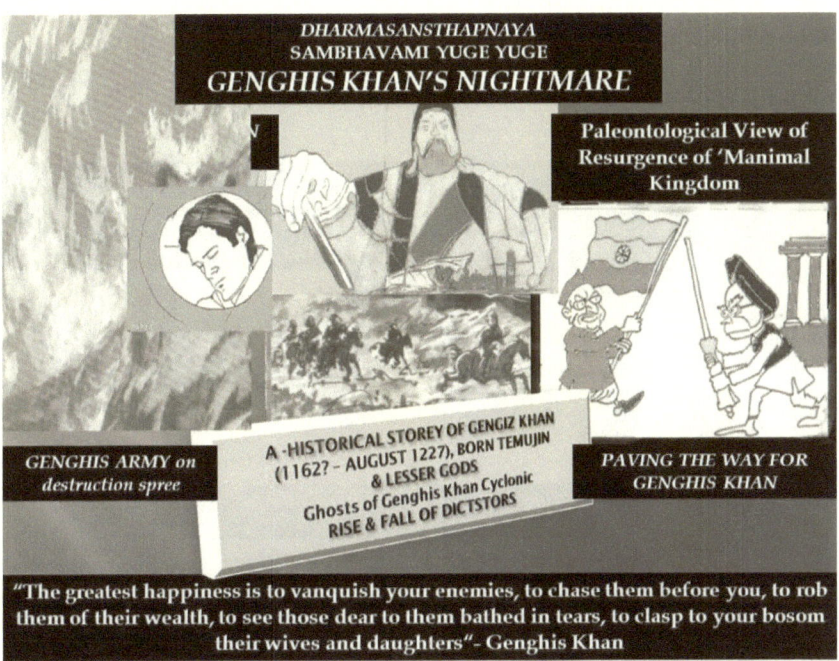

It's Genghis Khan's dream IN Indus valley. Under conditions of chaos and sleepiest night **the instincts from the hail** are stirred up by provoking events, awakened and surge ahead for their representation. In Henry Miller's words, **"current impression, some provoking occasion in the present which has been able to arouse one of the subject's major wishes"** Scene 1 shows Representations of **political sleep** and the **provoking political event**. Genghis Khan, the feared conqueror and repressor is again dreaming of one more conquests and the raging forces, represented by galloping stallions (male horses that have not been gelded- castrated), represent aggression and destructive rage, having assumed cyclonic scale. The dreams have their own logic of unfolding. Subsequent Scenes are couched with Super- Patriotic hate material and create frightening cinematic images. These are the creations of deep un-restful desires, activation of **traumatic fixation**, ever ready to spring into action, bring about **compression of images, condensation of past and present events**- memories. The unfolding Dream bellow is like a Socio-Political fiction, depiction of GENGHIS KHAN's frightening dream and which inevitably culminates on a **disastrous note, 'failure of Dream Work' (In Sigmund Freud's words)** of his famous dream- 'Red Blood on White Snow'. The Scene Two leads us into core of the deepest **oedipal desires r**esponsible for this Anxiety Dream.

SCENE 2

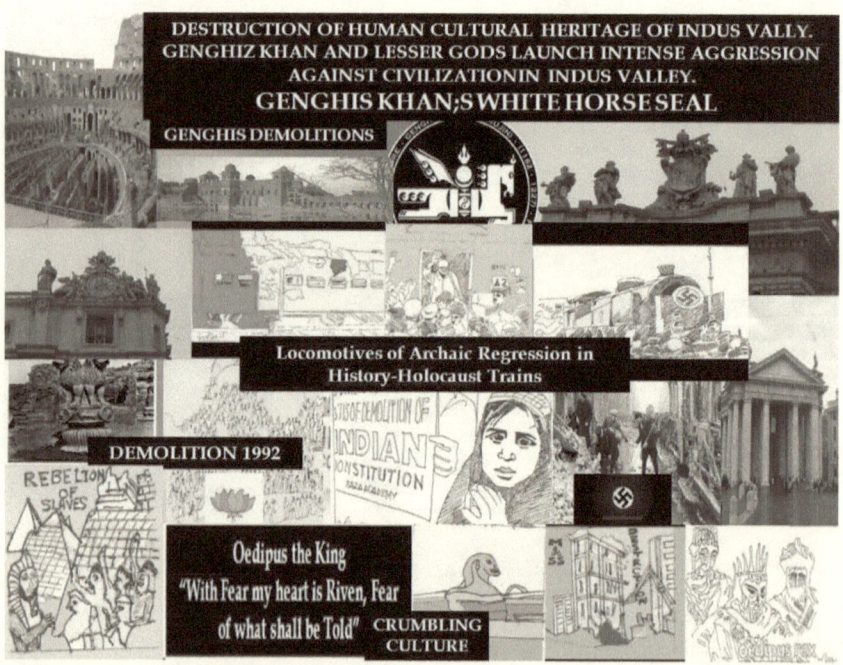

The dream SCENE 2-depicts the MULTIPLE IMAGES of regression to the archaic. Locomotives of regression (the burning train- leading into Nazism). However in the eyes of Psychoanalysts Genghis Khan's dreams are suspected to be grounded into Oedipus or Castration complex. The

metamorphosis of Instincts through genetic mutation of turn into violent mobs as expression from 'Within'. The critical – rational forces, intellectuals are plunged into another metamorphosis, Historians will see the myth of Genghis Khan playing out in dreams of all Fascist, Nazi or all right wing Dictators. By force of historical **logic, the dream re- travels on the same Foot Prints**. We will take a brief look at Genghis Storey. But the storey has **A-HISTORICAL Universal application in the eyes of Paleontologist or Psychoanalyst** both due to animalistic nature of the psychical forces of regression and demolitions of pluralistic cultures accomplished by them. The conditions of destruction of this Indus Civilization are laid -Down.

SCENE 3

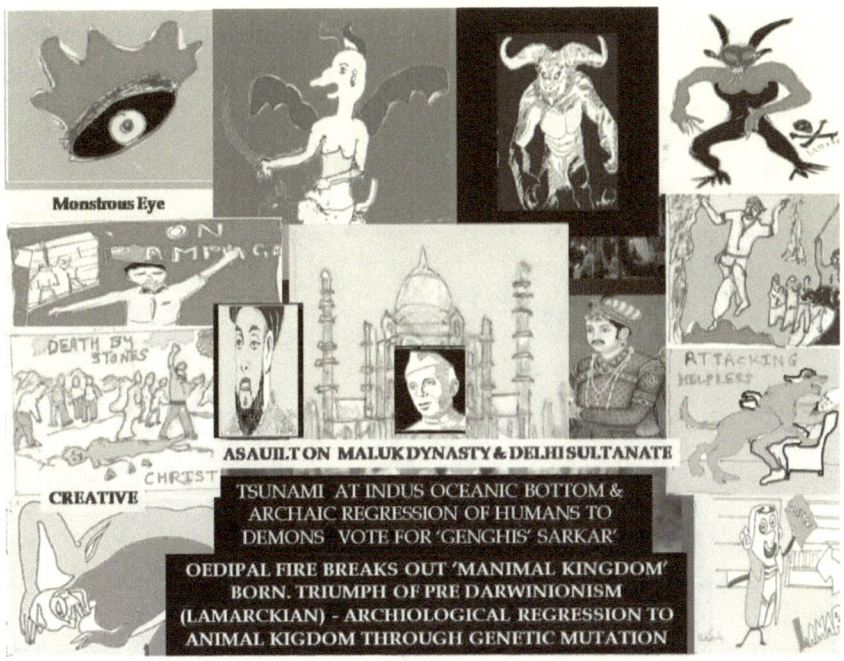

Mongol leader Genghis Khan conquered nearly 12 million square miles of territory—more than any individual in history. Along the way, he cut a ruthless path through Asia and Europe that left millions dead, **Genghis Brigades** have been known to be the cruelest and most feared ones and in zest to conquer, these Brigades drenched the enemy population in blood and continued even after GENGHIS KHAN's death. GENGHIS KHAN's rebirth marks rekindling of his regressive Oedipal desire to begin to launch devastating assault on the Secular Foundations of Delhi Sultanate, and Kill his HALF BROTHERS, remained unconquered from 12th to 21st Century. Psychoanalysis identifies it as **'PSYCHIC COMPULSION TO REPEAT'.** Regression to animal Kingdom and metamorphosis into Demons & manimals represents the street Fighters whose task is to follow the leaders and are not divided on class or creed lines. Despite Class ridden Society these demons are 'de-classed, Lumpen'. They are divided on Religious or sect lines. Their strength is **Sexual Fire, pure Instincts** aiming for attainment of Satisfaction.

Paleontologist and Psychoanalysts visualize this A- HISTORICAL storey of how the 'Oedipus Complex' influences the life of Human Groups on Carnage spree and crave for fulfillment of infantile wishes. These groups express their **common Neurosis, obsessions, psychosis, schizophrenia and phobia and multiple forms of psychological sicknesses**. Question is 'How far this Anxiety Dream will continue?

SCENE – 4

Scene Four represents the sharp escalation of GRIT of the Genghis Brigade which occupies the Center Stage of Socio Political situation. It represents **CONDENSATION** of all stages in History, from its **BOTTOM MOST** founding stages of SWASTIKA yesterday till blossoming rightwing today. Conspiracies, plots, intrigues and rioting played pivotal role in this escalation, in their assuming the **POLITICAL CENTRE STAGE**. Threats galore and outpour. Hate becomes the **WATCH WORD** and foams on to the top and Love and trust drowns into INDUS OCEAN. Intellectuals protest in vain, and creativity takes shelters into Paintings, Art and Literature. **Snake around the neck** represents symbolically the hate and fear together and is substitute, fetish of sexual desire. The hate and violence is disguised by the censorship in the explicit proclamation '**DHARMASANSTHAPANAY SAMBHAVAMI YUGE-YUGE**'.

SCENE – 5

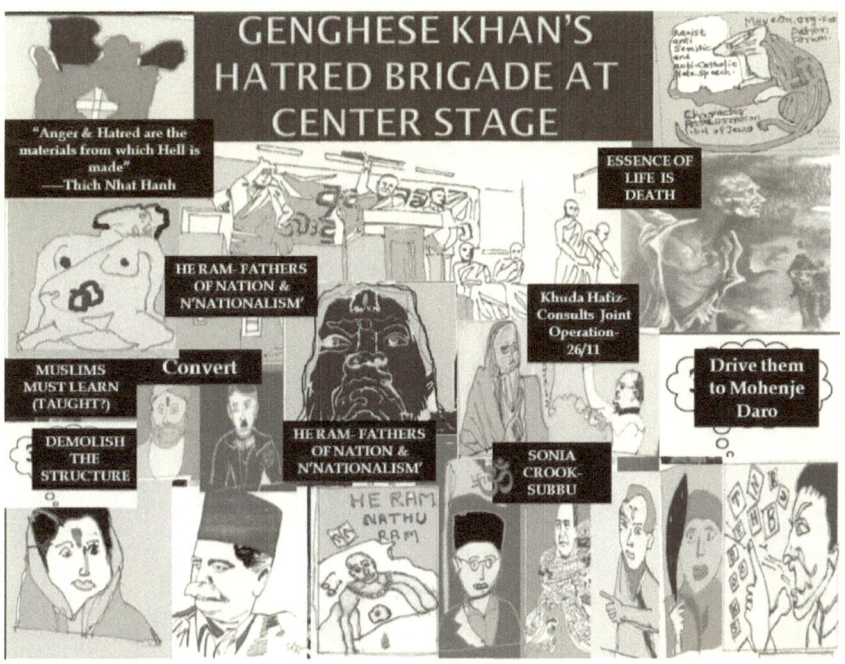

SCENE 5 drives the GENGHIS KHAN's dream into the background Image of a Cartoon used by Karl Polanyi, *The Great Transformation,* 1944, a critical commentary on Fascism and Liberal

Economics, which plays on 'Market Economics & Mechanism' which are directed at the fate of Human beings, the working classes and 'labor commodity'. Economic liberalism was **"kept open by an enormous increase in continuous, centrally organized and controlled interventionism'"**. He described it as 'FASCIST SITUATION" in which, "All at once, the tremendous industrial and political organizations of labor and of other devoted upholders of constitutional freedom would melt away".

This is exactly the situations which **dreams express or represent by similarities**, 'just as' or through metaphors. In Stephen Schettini words, **"Dreams are metaphors in Motion'**. Fascist situations are surprisingly identical to Franz Kafka's representations in METAMORPHOSIS and his other Novels and stories. Application of GENGHIS KHAN's Authoritarian Dream Rule combines- Applications of State Intervention at the behest of Corporate Capitalism at the cost of driving the transformation of human beings in to **"Warts'**.

SCENE -6

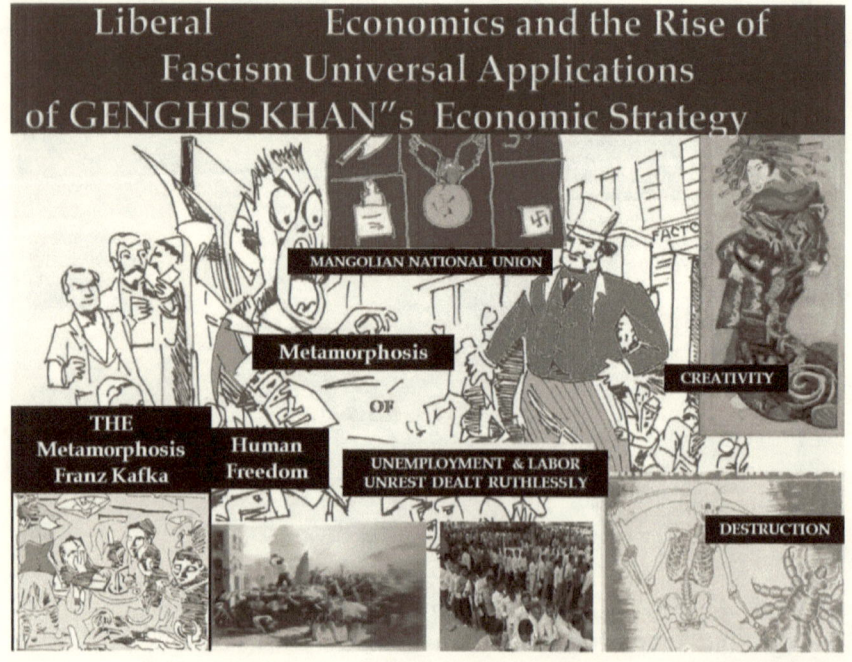

SCENE-6, brings us back to current SCENE 3, - Metamorphosis of difference classes of Humans into different creed of Manimals. The class of Humans, in possession of 'Means of Production, Exchange and Human Survival' are not street fighters, they work at Corridors of Political Powers. Their Greed metamorphoses them into Capitalist **Bulls, Bears and Bats** based in STOCK MARKET-EXCHANGES. They are named as **Capitalist Bullies- soft spoken Manimals- Cultured Class.** They ride on the backs of Street **Fighting Manimals** to GENGHIS KHAN but they are the Makers of KING GENGHIS KHAN. As ruling class they are in full command and control of the power-situation. They are the **real defenders of NATIONAL Interests.** They do not work on or trust in Caste or religious or communal lines and are SECULARS but **enjoy street fighting of the Non Secular street Fighting Demons.** They are INTERNATIONALISTS in so as far as their **GREED is** concerned but are truly Patriotic in their use of **BULLYING Power.** They are ruthlessly PATRIOTIC when it comes to 'use and throw' of labor commodity and in fullest exploitation of worker to increase the NATIONAL WEALTH. Exerting full repressive and crushing pressure on Labor, its organizations and **condescension of its history** by keeping the iron foot down to quell the resistance. Repression is ORDER of the DAY and thrust it down by Hook or Crook!

SLIDE 7

Scene Seven takes us to core of the rage, instigated by ruling Classes to gain absolute control over the economic, social & political situation and push the Expansionist strategy through aggression on enemy camps, flexing muscles and waging wars to annihilate enemy and to get sovereignty through mass enslavement.

Scholars estimate that GENGHIS KHAN may have killed a full three-fourths of modern-day Iran's population during his war with the Khwarezmid Empire. The extent of his Rage and cruelty is evident when It is said that Genghis killed many of the inhabitants, enslaved the rest, and executed Inalchuq, possibly by pouring molten gold or silver down his throat as retribution for the capture of the Mongol caravan.

In SCREEN Shot Seven we see Genghis believes in Oracle of 'Red Blood on white snow' and take to adventure of invading **TANGUT CITY OF RED WALL**. When it is believed that **'Everything is Fine'**, display of Corporate Development, progress and Military Might is on highest Scale or on high tide, the downslide **begins with rapid growth**

of clamor for War. The failure of the impulsive rage is round the corner. The fall out of the bankrupt Super Patriotic, Over ambitious strategy comes close.

SLIDE 8

Genghis expanse of the empire can be judged when it is said that, Genghis Khan's name "echoes through the history of Europe and Asia with a drumbeat of horse-Hoovers accompanied by screams of doomed townspeople". **Genghis Khan. Is regarded as the 'Man who almost destroyed Islam". Genghis Khan attacked the Turko-Persian Muslim Khwarazmian empire of Samarkand avenged the attacks launched by the Arab and Persian Muslims in to Tartary (Central Asia).** The amorphous mass of dejected and frustrated people are spellbound by opium of **'CHARISMA' of GENGHIS** and would rise to the occasion to lead his people to new victories to fulfill his own Dreams of 'United INDUS". Genghis quickly came into conflict with the Jin Dynasty of the Jurchens and the Western Xia of **TANGUTS** in northern China. He dealt ruthlessly with other Powers and dreamt of creating vast empire by invading TIBET, Russia, Belarus, Persia,

Ukraine, Khwarezmia and Eastern Iran. The empire, Redish-Safron, grew rapidly, in every direction, becoming largest ever transcontinental empire connecting the East & West.

Historically his Empire was the largest in size and his ambitions were the wildest and finally achieved to create the expanded EMPIRE encompassing Magolia, Parts of China, Russia, Large chunks of India and intruded deep into Europe. His followers,. The expanse of his empire surpasses that of NEPOLIAN, ALEXANDER or MUSSOLINI and ADOLF HITLER and currently the lesser gods, surging forward in Indus Valley.

SLIDE 9

Scene Nine shows Scenes of despair. Dream Image of aggression on TANGUT- Central China, leads to total despair at home front. Defeat of GENGHIS KHAN is imminent. The intense sexual desire once again driving him (compulsion to repeat) to capture **Central China-TANGUT and which transforms the NIGHTMARE-in to 'Truth'.** When the desire fails to reach satisfaction, it results in to failure of function of dream work, reaches the flash point' the breakdown of dream and awakening from slumber for mass of people, becomes imminent. It begins playing havoc on streets. Labor regimentation and forced labour is at peak. The reins of power begin tottering and to retain political control mass annihilation begins like the one under Nazi holocaust. The prayers of Fathers of nation and the ordinary man on streets fall on deaf ears, go unheard and Melancholia and Mourning represents the order of the day.

SLIDE 10

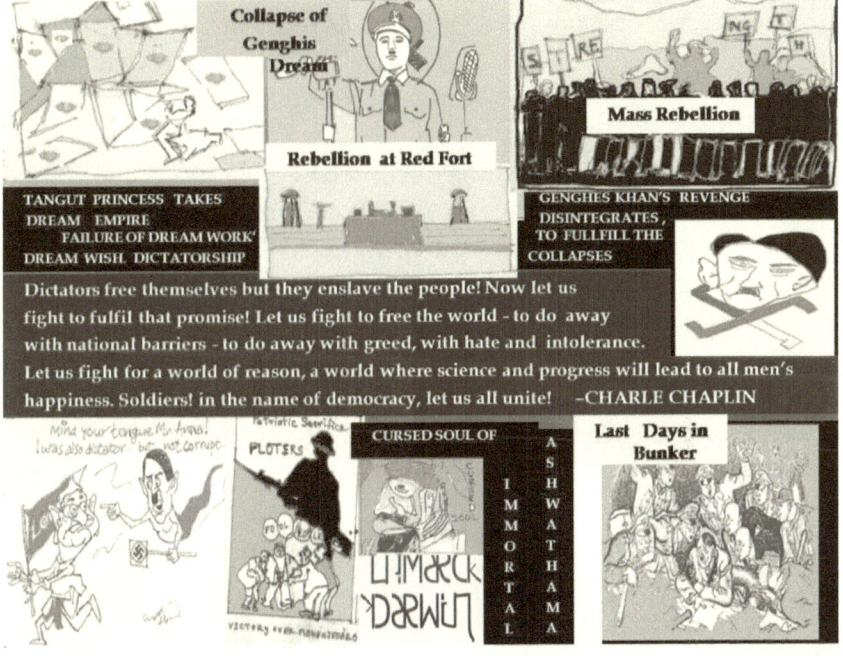

Scene Ten. The collapse of Rage of HATRED BRIGADES and Storm Troopers, ambitious Visions of expansion of 'UNITED INDUS VALLY", the horrendous mass rage in civilized world is decisively concluded in the last Scene. Sir David Low has expressed this collapse while Charlie Chaplin introduces the mass rebellion from within the ranks and file of disciplined soldiers, from the electrifying enlightenment of the working classes regimented through repression. The spirited speech of this prodigy from the ramparts of **REDFORT** brings forward hope for Humanity, for world of science and progress overcoming the National Boundaries. The rebellion impinges on the images as disturbing stimulus. **The rule of HATE, Role of Bulls, rule at Gun Point and strangulation of Justice** Breaks down and ends. **Annaji who provided the stimulus to Rage** and Dictators are on the run and are trapped in inescapable situation. Worried NAZIS spend their last Nights of collapse in Encapsulated closed Bunkers. The Dream Ends and finally common man, once relived, says, **"IT WAS ONLY A DREAM".** It requires Charlie Chaplin to play the double role, one as Dictator and other as LIBERATOR to tie up the Latent and manifest contents of the Anxiety Dream.

Contemporary economic-socio-political situation reminds us the integration of Sigmund Freud and Jean Batiste Lamarck. Reality is established at the end of Ten Scenes or Screen Shots by the upsurge of working masses (soldiers) breaking up of the PHANTASY. This Story of GENGHIS KHAN which has Universal Applications and repeats itself, in every century and each Age begins fading with SUNRISE of morning hours, the **UPSURGE IN MASS AWAKENING.** We hope that this storey will come to an end and bring world piece for all times and allow **Genghis Khan** to escape from Oedipal –Castration Curse of TANGUT Princess, that unless **he overcomes his castration complex and resolves the conflict between his super ego and instincts,** he will continue to have never ending Horror Dream and painful end. The Dream story can be likened to Lord Krishna's curse to **Ashwatthama, that "for 3000 Years** he will roam in the forests with blood and puss oozing out of his injuries and cry for death but even death would not have mercy on him".

(Thanks to My Creative Cartoonist Friend, Mr. Sriniwas Prabhudesai who contributed with most of the cartoon Images used in the Ten collages used as unfolding of Dream of Genghis Khan. The images have been subjected to laws of dream work, namely distortion compounding, displacement and disguise! The Screen Play however has surely answered one question; does the Dream Play predict the future? It has been long ago answered by Sigmund Freud, "By representing a wish as fulfilled the dream certainly leads us into the future; but this future, which the dreamer accepts as his present, has been shaped in the likeness of the past by the indestructible wish")

References:-

In the Footsteps of Ghengis Khan- <u>**John DeFrancis**</u>

The great transformation-Karl Polanyi

The Metamorphosis – Franz Kafka

ARTICLE II

DAVID LOW'S LEGACY AND SIGMUND FREUD

A Jewish refugee from Vienna, a very old man personally unknown to you, cannot resist the impulse to tell you how much he admires your glorious art and your inexorable, unfailing criticism.- SIGMUND FREUD. (Letter to Sir David Low)

"Art does not reside in the materials nor the subject-matter. It resides in the artist". "I was an artist who drew politics, not a politician who drew pictures. Public affairs were the raw material for my drawing and I had no wish to 'get on' in politics. Although I sought famous people for professional reasons", (Sir David Low- Autobiography)

My curiosity of in what way Sir David Low defines as relationship between 'Artist and his Art' led me to write up this expository write up. I can begin by quoting highlights from Sir David Low's Autobiography. "I was seventeen and growing up. As things were then in New Zealand there was an economic inevitability about my gravitation towards political cartooning. Illustrating jokes would never keep me. Caricaturing personalities offered very limited prospects. But here was a regular job at which, with freelancing additions, I could make a living. Up till then I had been interested mainly in the drawing, and not in drawing my opinions. Now I had to take a closer interest in public affairs. I started as the **obedient hireling,** but after a time, *when I got into the swing of it, naturally my own political inclinations began to creep into the cartoons,* proving once again that *matter and manner of artistic expression are one,* and irony and sarcasm are difficult to harness".

• David Low's cartoonish demonstrate his opinions, inclinations and responses to the rise of European Dictators and the rapid passage to Second World War and which proved to be defining moments in shaping the popular opinions and inspiring resistance to dictatorships in political and social life. He inherited the legacy of Thomas Nast, the founder of American political cartoonist, who fought for abolition of slavery, racial discrimination, white supremacy, Nationalism and anti- immigration violence. David Low formed the continuity with 'Anti War', anti imperialist radical cartoonist Robert Minor but avoided Robert Minor's mistake of surrendering his Art to politics! He continued to be part of liberal, democratic tradition in usage of the power of 'political cartoon'. He proactively developed insights into the future course of events which Hitler led the world to most destructive Global war. He targeted the dictators including Adolf Hitler and his counter parts in Italy, Russia and Spain through his innovative *cartoon campaigns.* He drove Hitler to extreme irritation and wilderness. As a brilliant 'Political' cartoonist strategist he could educate the masses against the dangers of 'Appeasements' policies and innovatively upheld the 'liberal and popular democracy'. My interest in Sir David Low is confined to his opinions, his Artistic expression and the relevance they have today.

David Low's Aims- Innovative "Nuisance dedicated to Sanity'

It is not that Cartoonish as an Art flourished in one quarter. There is another quarter which enslaved this Art form – which formed a distinct repressive tradition- Fascist. This tradition has understood, not the creative and revolutionary aspects of this Art Form but, usage of this subversive Art as a tool of propaganda in promoting 'prejudice' and fantasy and using the intensity expressed through Cartoon for whacking the opponents, the 'Anti national enemies '! The peculiar ground, 'prejudice' on which their Art Form is built can be illustrated by Joseph Goebbels' quote. **"It was often easier to express NAZI ideas in a political cartoon than with the written word. A cartoon would express concepts in a quickly understood manner that was impossible to attain in an article"**- From- 'Goebbels and Der Angriff' (The paper founded by Joseph Goebbels in 1926)

Sir David Low harnessed his Art as a critique of the popular 'prejudices' and those of the political leadership of the British establishment. His cartoon character, Colonel Blimp made the highest impact in shaping the 'opinion'. Blimp represented a 'fascistoid' stereotype character and everything Sir David Low disliked in British politics. David Low says, "Blimp was no enthusiast for democracy. He was impatient with the common people and their complaints. His remedy to social unrest was less education, so that people could not read about slumps. An extreme isolationist, disliking foreigners (which included Jews, Irish, Scots, Welsh, and people from the Colonies and Dominions); *a man of violence, approving war"*.

Sir David Low is described as the greatest cartoonist of all times. 'Political cartoon gallery' says, "Low created many memorable characters, including the Two-headed Ass, the TUC carthorse, and Colonel Blimp. Describing himself as 'a nuisance dedicated to sanity' Low was a hugely influential cartoonist and caricaturist, producing over 14,000 drawings during the course of his 50 year career".

Researcher and Founder of the Political Cartoon Gallery from Bloomsbury Dr. Timothy Benson, states, "Sir David Low (1891-1963) was probably the most celebrated political cartoonist of the last century. He is best remembered today for the way he mercilessly ridiculed in a humorous vein the dictators, Hitler and Mussolini during the 1930s. Despite several attempts to censor him, Low fought an almost personal war against Hitler and the Nazis which was played out for all to see in the pages of the Evening Standard. Michael Foot, who was Acting Editor on the Evening Standard from 1938, felt that Low's attacks on Hitler met with considerable success. 'Low contributed more than any other single figure and as a result changed the atmosphere in the way people saw Hitler. Other cartoonists did not have such a long-standing record."

Dr. Timothy who profusely admired David Low's Cartoon Campaigns and analyzes Sir David Low's propelling motives and desires. "Low's humanitarian instincts and Liberal upbringing gave him a strong determination to oppose Hitler and everything he stood for. It would be Low's depiction of Hitler, above all others, that most got under the Fuhrer's skin. Consequently, the Nazis even tried, in 1937, to put pressure on the British Government to restrain Low from satirizing Hitler in his cartoons. This only bolstered Low's reputation as an independent operator at the Evening Standard, especially when it was well-known that he worked for a proprietor such as Lord Beaverbrook, who was a consistent and staunch supporter of Chamberlain's 'Appeasement policy'.

David Low was not the stooge or hireling of the 'ruling class' and ignored "the warning and continued to deride the Nazi regime. "Evening Standards felt that Low's concentration on Hitler had become too frequent and may appear to readership of the Evening Standard as a vendetta against the German Dictator". In November 1936, the editor, Percy Cudlipp, (with Beaverbrook's sanctions) refused to publish 'THE JAW IS THE JAW OF MUSSO, BUT" and subjected' cartoon campaigns against 'dictators' to censorship of 'responsibilities' under 'The present international situation'. David Low did not buckle under the 'censorship' and 'repression'. In his brilliant Article Dr. Timothy Benson narrates the storey. "The Nazi hierarchy seemed to have been particularly incensed by Low's cartoon strip 'Hit and Muss', which had been appearing weekly in his full page 'Topical Budget' from October 1937' and exercised intense, pressure on German political establishment to compel Sir David Low to shelve his campaign. Before out break out of War with Germany, the appeasement of German Dictator was still the order of the day. Struggling to resist, wriggle out from this 'undeclared' censorship, undeterred by the ban on his cartoons in

Italy, Spain and Germany, he continued his cartoon campaign. He was an innovative solution finder and without compromise ultimately, he discovered the highly innovative idea of creating a composite dictator named 'Muzzler', (controlling, repressing, preventing from expressing) by fusing well-known features of both dictators (Mussolini and Hitler) 'without being identifiable as either'. It **made** its appearance on pages of Evening Standard on 1st January 1938. As the Article points out the name was certainly intended "as a pun to show how the authorities had unsuccessfully attempted to muzzle the cartoonist".

However curiosity will lead us to look beyond 'Muzzler as an artistic expression and search for genesis of it as a form arising out of compression of several thought processes or a 'composite figure', a structure as a form of expression employed to disclose and mask their identity at the same time in order to hoodwink the muzzling repressive mental agencies. I will explore this point explaining the affinity between Sir David Low and Sigmund Freud in next section.

Cartoons, Dream condensation & Art of Interpretation!

Sir David Low's interest in observing the objects on the move was prolific and that sprung from his interest in drawing 'Comic Strips'. (1903)

Eger to make 'representation of life' in the drawings David Low felt the need to study the objects on the move. "What I needed was a series of busts of Homer sitting in a row, each wearing a different expression, so that I could study the characteristic disturbance of features in the acts of laughing, crying, sneezing, etc. I needed a real life class with a moving model, so that I could closely observe just what happens when one walks, and just what one can and cannot do with arms and legs ; a class for drawing from memory at which I could crystallize my impressions; a class for the analysis of character"- David Low.

In these remarks we see David Low, not only as a 'cinematographer' and character-logist and but also an Art Interpreter and a researcher. He intended to make alive emotional and physical movements of the objects in a cartoon which are then *frozen into sculptures*! Here we are reminded of interpretation of aesthetical works by Sigmund Freud, Moses of Michelangelo in which he discovers all possible emotional, psychological and physical movements frozen into the sculpture. Though both of them approached the 'Object' from opposite directions, both of them became the interpreters. Both researched into the gestural and 'automatist' qualities the caricature, cartoon, sculpture and dream images which invoke and communicate to audience or viewers the 'unconscious associations'. Hence of both of them aimed at uncovering the mechanisms of crystallized images and their dissemination by 'large audience'.

Sir David Low had learnt long back techniques to anticipate responses to his cartooning by 'intolerant' dictators and censoring agencies! Storey of his encounters with dictators and repression goes back to his struggle against similar attempted muzzling and repression by the then Australian Prime Minister Mr. Hughes, who formed the anti –Labor' "National Government in 1911. David Low's anti- war cartoons published in 'Bulletin' targeted the *'dominating Personality'*, DP, through a series of cartoons. David Low says, "The press had began to wilt under censorship pressure" from the PM Mr. Billy Hughes. PM's personal threats and instructions to muzzle the cartoon campaign have been vividly narrated by him. "My cartoons reflected this view week by week by featuring Billy carrying a penny balloon inscribed CD.P.5 for *Dominating Personality*". *David Low's 'Muzzler' has its origins in his cartoon DP.* David Low makes an interesting comment on this incident. "I had a charmed life with Censors until one day Billy's vanity exploded". Fortunately Editor of Bulletin supported David Low.

'Muzzler' demonstrates that Sir David Low had become wiser and learnt something extraordinary from his experience on 'DP'. There are reasons to believe that Sir David Low was a keen observer of his own dreams. Given the fact that David Low suffered from periodic insomnia and struggled a lot for a solution, in this context, his revelation becomes important. "The Lows were always night birds. Whatever time I got up, I was never properly awake". This gives clues to origins of his great Cartoon Images. The Dream images became closest ally and assistant of this great creative Artist, who relied upon, 'unconscious' springs of thoughts, images, which when released busted asunder the yoke of psychic repression during sleep with full force. Artist's other ally, was of course was the trained ego, critical faculties, which translated these stream of *condensed images* 'otherwise inaccessible' to waking consciousness' into Works of Art!

Sigmund Freud notices how dream utilizes the relation of similarity, metaphor, or the `just-as.` Freud calls this the primary foundations of dream construction. It is assisted by the mechanism of condensation (see pp. 383ff) in two ways: [1] through identification with singular persons-- i.e., in terms of names, physical characteristics, gestures, understanding; and [2] *composition--of both things and persons--where two separate objects are condensed together.* (432) In his Dream Book, Sigmund Freud calls it 'composite figure. Because either the things or the persons are unified they become accessible to the dream contents without the censor interfering. Thus, it may be said that condensation satisfies the claims of the dream censor.

Freud then refers to *composite structures.* These structures are represented [1] one thing which accompanies the knowledge that specific attributes of the dream thought belong to another dream thought. [2] Or through the combination of features of the two dream thoughts to form a new image. Freud notes, that is the construction is too large, the dream is content to represent one part distinctly and the other vaguely.

Again, In 1916, in 'Wit and its relation to Unconscious' Sigmund Freud discusses the intent and function of caricature in expressing 'Rebellion Against Authority Through Wit'. "The prevention of abuse or insulting retorts through outer circumstances is so often the case that tendency-wit is used with special preference as a weapon of attack or criticism of superiors who claim to be an authority. Wit then serves as a resistance against such authority and as an escape from its pressure. In this factor, too, lies the charm of caricature, at which we laugh even if it is badly done simply because we consider its resistance to authority a great merit".

'Muzzler' is just one illustration. We find innumerable cartoons from David low *stamped like condensed images*. For illustration, 3 rd July 1934 cartoon with caption reading- **"They salute with both hands, now!"** http://www.slideshare.net/DHUMPHREYS/night-of-the-long-knives) (Cartoon Item No. 2085- The British cartoon Achieves). This

David Low cartoon shows Hitler holding the smoking gun and Goering (shown as Thor, the God of War- derived from mythology) Cartoon Interpreters have exactly identified the significance of "glowering at - not the traditional Nazi salute - but terrified SA men *with their hands up.* Some SA men already lie dead on the ground. Goebbels is shown as Hitler's poodle". Low portrays Hitler as a brazen murderer keeping his men in check by naked fear. More importantly such cartoons perused the historical truth and the psychical essence of the events powerfully and brilliantly. Kind of emotional, psychological impact the cartoon makes on the viewers in empathetically evoking the human pain, terror and pathos from the depths of their psyche is incomparable. The effects have become possible because of condensation of several images of historical *events have been casted into a single humorous cartoon image.*

David Low's cartoons after cartoons exhibit the same quality with consistency and has become the backbone of his greatness and uniqueness. Hence Sigmund Freud calls these qualities as 'inexorable unfailing criticism'. Naturally Freud was elated with empathy, to witness proof of reflections of his own discovery and discoveries in David Low's Art of cartooning, understanding of mechanisms of 'dream work'. Condensation and creation of composite images is hallmark of tricks played by 'dream work'. I guess Sigmund Freud must have been delighted to see such outstanding works of Art. Sigmund Freud had discovered and exhaustively discussed the techniques adopted by dreams in representing multiplicity of 'unconscious' and 'pre conscious' thought processes through *construction of collective and composite images.* He identifies them as "the principal methods of dream-condensation". Both these greats discovered them independently, though Freud was the first to put it into psychoanalytic theory. Sigmund Freud's Victorian aesthetical tastes were in congruence with those of Sir David Low.

There are innumerable cartoons from these creative Artists which can be identified as products of such condensations of several strands of thought processes. Cartoons of this type have been subjected to multiple brilliant interpretations. Cartoon remains the only Art Form capable of 'speaking' the buried truth. It reveals the truth of Chinese Proverb, 'A picture is worth of thousand words'. In tiniest and compact form evokes humor, comic and human pathos. Hence Sigmund Freud's appreciated this 'glorious Art' which launches criticism by exaggerating the absurdities, creates 'real' in the form of phantasm by combining and juxtaposing the irreconcilable (at times) opposites and reaches out to viewers innermost core of psychic being..

'That depends on the aim of the prejudice.' David Low.

During his official visit to Soviet Union in 1929, David Low had an interesting conversation with the Polish born talented, one time, Russian Revolutionary Karl Radek, (the son of Jewish parents, born in Luxemburg 1885. He capitulated to Stalin in 1927 but met with the same fate as the great Revolutionary Leon Trotsky, assassination at the hands of Stalinist in 1939). Karl Radek was one brilliant propagandist of the Bolsheviks from first Russian revolution of 1905. Karl Radek was then the Press chief and supreme boss of Soviet propaganda.

"We talked of propaganda, the techniques of persuasion, emphasis and diminution, the comparative effectiveness of statement and parable, soothing expressions and the exciting expression, shock or tickle in the use of words and images. It came to this: it all depends upon the receptivity of the audience. You have to stay within its range of pick-up; otherwise you are talking to yourself. 'Now, that's where pictures have an advantage, said he. 'Not really,' I said, 'Much the same limitations. All right if you stick to trite simplicity and traditional symbolic forms. But if you want to extend and bring your picture-language up to date, it's an educational job of labeling and impressing new association's reiteration and repetition.' 'I always look at the cartoons in a newspaper first, he said. 'They tell me how things are. Your medium is no good for plain statement, but it is ideal for creating prejudice.

'Sounds immoral,' said I, knowing better.

'Oh, no,' he said. 'That depends on the aim of the prejudice.'. *'Supposing your aim is to weaken prejudice and provoke people to use their own brains?'. Someone spirited him away and our*

Pleasant talk ended in the air.

The conversation speaks volumes about the cartoon and caricature as a form of Art and the potentials it carries to work as double edged sword in either provoking people to 'think' or to create prejudice. Cartoonists create 'stereotypes' characters to achieve their goals and define their targets, as vehicle of mass communication and for provoking viewers.

Sir David Low created the character 'Colonel Blimp', a character to project an imaginative, stereotype (Lord Blimp, Bishop Blimp, Dr. Blimp, Mr. Blimp etc.) to reflect and represent the virtues and prejudices of the viewers' in 1930's Europe. *A thought provoking stereotype to educate the people and weaken the prejudice*! Soon Colonel Blimp became the 'public property' talked about everywhere for years together!

On the other hand we have in India number of Cartoonists who have attempted to create their stereotype! Most of the cartoonists could not avoid temptation of drawing Muslim community, en lot, over years. Community has been stereotyped and symbolically represented through cartoons. It is given the 'look' of a classical 'butcher, killer of 'cows and human beings all alike'. The man and his symbolic attire, wearing a 'Lungi'. Other prominent features of the Muslim, like wearing the 'skull cap', dirty, unshaven, starkly half naked, figure with protruding belly and ruthless facial expression. This is the devised Propped up, imagery of Muslim to target the Hindu psyche and has been played very well, in different situations and as response to minor and major events with some variations to promote 'prejudice' and fearful 'castration complex'

Such cartoons have become the plank for bashing the Muslim community and generate hatred. Sch underground campaign against Muslims Community and 'Islam' in 1960's, 1990s and subsequently provided opportunity for emergence as rescuer and messiah of Hindutwa and target the 'collaborators' of 'anti nationals' as dirty, uncultured and hateful. *Patriotism* was ruse, superb outward expression while prejudices were on the boil at the bottom promoting violence.

Sir David Low stereotyped Colonel Blimp to represent sum total of popular prejudices to 'weaken' them and provoke people to think, Stereotyping of Muslim was to strengthen the popular prejudices and stop people to 'think'. It gives us insights into what Sir David Low meant by, when he says, *'That depends on the aim of the prejudice.'*

Archaic Symbolic Violence and stereotyping in Cartoonish.

Cartoon as Art form comprehends and integrates several art forms such as Drawings and paintings on one hand and literature on the other hand because of its ability to express the 'un spoken- pictorial- visual and the written word' *in symbolic, distorted and condensed form*. Like dreams, it uses distortion displacement, condensation, dramatization, and secondary elaboration as mechanisms for representation of individuals, historical circumstaces and political events. However it has all the possibilities to pierce into the region called political imagery but *differs from dreams* due to its great potentials to be *intelligible and real which is achieved by Artist through mental work of expression*. It carries within it the virtues of interpretation to 'unmask' and 'degrade' and thus to challenge the 'in tolerance' of self proclaimed authority.

Characteristics of Fascist Political Cartoonist work differs from the work of 'free thinker' because their cartoonish shows no or limited capacity to work on 'condensation of thought processes' at the disposal of Artist' and instead takes easy recourse to obsessive symbolism. Hence it enslaves this Art form and subjugates it to expression of 'prejudice' which s expressed symbolically. Two important aspects of 'dream work' which it could utilize and are at its disposal are 'distortion' (which was life of caricatures), 'displacement' and symbolic representation in directing the energies stored in imagery on to the 'Other'. These characteristics of unconscious expression achieves the delivery of *personal* anger, hatred, fear or terror and archaic violence on to the viewers effectively.

Fascist and Nazi cartooning thrives on defending its violence as 'counter violence' against stereotyped community. Opponents; Jews and Marxists as evils and are often symbolically portrayed as venomous-poisonous 'serpents', snakes or demons. The Pamphlet, 'Killing the Jews in Nazi Propaganda' by Randall Bytwerk's 'Nazi Symbolic Violence' reproduces cartoon captioned "Don't let it Go' (1935) poisonous snake in the stubborn and quelling powerful grip of German hand prompting the viewers not to let it go, not allow the serpent to escape and ensure that it strangled to death and killed to liberate German people from the misery imposed by Jews and Marxists. Indian Fascist cartoonists also have taken great pride in portraying Child Lord Krishna Killing the

Demon, the deadly Poisonous Cobra serpent 'Kalia' residing in river Yamuna to quell the poisonous opponents and Muslims.

Killing the 'poisonous snake' provides justification of violence as 'counter violence' in retaliation because it is poisonous! Affectivity of snake symbol lies in its ability to utilize the unconscious, archaic 'dread of the snake' to awaken and foster hysteria and obsessive neurosis of the viewers and create hysteric groups. Any interpreter will understand that snake is disguised representation of 'male organ' and invokes castration complex articulated as neurotic and hysterical symptoms.

Another means at the disposal of Fascist cartoonists is targeting the enemy community by it's symbolic stereotyping as oppressor! 1924 Poster-Cartoon shows the Stereotyped bald headed fat Jew, with protruding tummy and wearing pompous suit riding on the shoulders of stout German. Jew is holding fast in left hand the shackles fastened in the mouth of the enslaved German and is being driven with the whip in the right hand. The poster is titled "Down with Financial Enslavement! Vote National Socialist!" (1924). Cartoons of these types were repeated in Joseph Goebbels's Berlin weekly 'Der Angriff'.

Political Cartoonist in India also towed the same stereotyped symbolism and have fanatically propagated the same message. We come across few typical cartoons showing Muslim community symbolized by shabby-look, wearing a skull cap and protruding belly and this man (Muslim), falling over a frail Hindu symbolizing "the burden of increasing Muslim population on Hindus in India".

Promoting medieval legends for the justification of 'counter violence' or instigation for it is significant theme of these Indian or other cartoonists. Jews, Muslims and labor leaders shown as 'stone aged' or frightening demon holding thorny weapon with bones of Hindus or opponents scattered around, suggesting as being guilty of mass murders and slaughters. For projecting widespread Jewish violence against Germans, Medieval legends of ritual murder promoting rumors were used to claim that Jews frequently murdered Christians to secure their blood for religious purposes. Such instigative cartoons promote hysteric hatred against 'others'.

In contrast, we can see Sir David Low's outstanding popular cartoon 'RENDEZOUS' (Evening Standard, 20 th Sept. 1939, Item LSE 2692, www.cartoons.ac.uk/record/LSE2692), also shows violence to provoke us to think. The cartoon is drawn on the background of joint invasion of Poland by Adolf Hitler and Joseph Stalin, greeting each other with pride, at the site of generic dead body of the human race (Or polish people) with pleasure and pride, *'scum of the earth' and 'bloody assassin of workers'* both killers showing smug over the killing. The cartoon provokes us to empathize with the generic body. Theese cartoons define the conflict of two confronting trends within cartoonish world of Art.

Master Stroke for all Ages

History will recognize Sir David Low, not only as Humanitarian Humorist and cartoonist with extra ordinary wit but more importantly he was essentially an 'anti war' activist! Sir *David Low\Cornell Blimp' aimed at disrupting and des-respected popular beliefs since they were "all too often popular prejudices and were nearly always founded upon undue respect or reverence for someone or something*. The very essence of satire was disrespect and irreverence". He had closely observed the disasters during the world war I and Colonel Blimp "made me a sturdy democrat, considerate of the condition of the common people; for more education; for international co-operation; holding war, per se, as bad; for the League of Nations and united efforts to build a sane international system; for economic reorganization of world resources to that end; for piping down national arms". He used all his powers as humorist against 'war-mongers' and against the dictators.

His Anti War poster, "Progress of Man 1935 AD' is stinging critique of Fascism, Nationalism- Patriotism' and depicts the 'regression of man' to dark ages of cannibalism'. The conversation between the pig and the naked *'cylindrical mouthed gas masked'* man, resembling pig, bending forward to become four legged animal, visually depicting his ancestral animal origins. Pig says, "they kill me to eat, but you poor sap, they kill you for your own good". The comments were intended to provoke the blind followers of Nazi ideology to think. ". (http://www.cartoons.ac.uk/ search/cartoon_item/progress of man1935 ad) or (View cartoon item: LSE2191). It was a message to the masses *to wake up and understand* the 'mass psychology of fascism" and awaken the blinded poor mass following of the fascists dictators from their slumber to realize their own status as the 'four legged masked animal-man'. It depicts their prejudices, regression and blindness. This painful but educative snub to 'war mongers' has become the symbolic representation and a master stroke of all ages.

Origins, Aims, Objectives and historicity in Sir David Low's Art of Cartoonish

David Low versatility as cartoonish is embedded in 'Aims and Objectives' of his Art of cartoonish. He integrated three founding aims and elements of this Art. As comics, he delivered his excellent humorous observations addressed to common man. As a social cartoonist, he grasped fundamental inexorable demands on life of common man, his problems, his hardships and inhuman conditions of his life and hence always aimed for humane **'objectivity'**. Thirdly, as a rebellion, **against social-political** orthodoxy, repression and authoritarianism he had 'political' aim, to communicate partisan message to viewers. It was to 'provoke' them to think, draw, attract them to his views and designed to influence them to respond to specific political events or circumstances in a manner the Cartoonist sees and interprets. Hence his aims were greater than those of journalists or writer and came close to those of a critical impartial historian, to objectively analyze and interpret. David Low's aim of cartooning was aimed at criticism and criticism. As an Artist he used humor and comics as the means and medium of Interpretation to activate viewers' responses.

David Low's experience made him into a complete 'character-logistic' and sharply differentiated him-self from cartoonists whose aim could be downright malicious. An Artist by birth, 'psychologist' by habit and historian made by penetrative restless enthusiasm and hard work, he made his mark when he says, "those with only the vulgar conception of caricature as aimless *distortion of physical shortcomings could have had no inkling of my own view of it.* How could I have explained my eagerness to find its art, my zest to try to capture and *reduce to visual terms that most elusive of all qualities, individuality* ?". He adds up,

"A good piece of caricature represents not only what the artist sees but *what he knows about what he draws".*

Exploring the techniques of creating character, David Low says, "I would try a set of portraits. None of that clever superficial stuff 'in a few brilliant lines.' None of that easy exaggeration of physical peculiarities merely, 1 would aim at carrying each subject a stage or two further towards *fuller and more rounded representation.* This time I would go to infinite trouble. No time limit deep observation, minute perception, *Analysis and synthesis of character".* These lines can come from a brilliant 'psychologist' and complete Artist only. He says, "I was aware that my own efforts had been, to say the worst, catch-as-catch-can, to say the best, unorthodox, in that my search for knowledge had usually *begun at the apex and worked back to the base, from effect to cause, from current affairs to historical origins, instead of the other way round".*

He explored the circumstances and events in depths to provide full representation to the Characters. He used both the techniques of disguising and unmasking the characters, without compromising on criticism and ridiculing. David Low hints at 'disguising' techniques used in Greek Comedy in which "the actors wearing masks are turned into caricatures of living politicians and other nuisances. That was to be my department". In Australia Sir David Low's techniques were influenced and shaped by Will Dyson and Norman Lindsay. Dyson's cartoons used to represent War and Destruction by symbols of Devil, used to represent Finance Capital and Power by 'Fat' symbol popular amongst working class and image of greed by large figure with paunch, top hat, spats and a cigar. *This political philosophical influence never left David Low nor he was lured by any temptation to cross the boundaries of Art to peruse political ambitions.*

India had produced 'Political Cartoonists' who drew 'KAMAJIS' and 'BAWAJIS' to represent 'common man' at the beginning of their careers, claimed to have been mentored by Sir David Low but in Sir David Low's words all of them ended up by becoming **'politicians' who drew pictures'.** Blinded by personal political ambitions they lost sight of Sir David Low's heritage, his humanitarian, psychological, philosophical and his Artistic aims and objectives. *Opposed to the* *historical methodology' of Sir David Low,* they saw all 'Current affairs' through the prism of prejudices, projected 'medieval symbols' to unveil their own autocratic ambitions and programs, lost 'objectivity' and inquisitiveness to find the historical origins of events, played into the hands of blind historical forces of reaction and shook hands not with Sir David Low but his 'Cornel Blimp'.

Sir David Low was a product of a tradition of critical Art which he inherited and never lost sight of bright revolutionary history which brought him the fame as critical Artist. In modern times, Leonardo da Vinci (1452 -1519) and his artistic explorations of "the ideal type of deformity' the grotesque truly discovered it *as form of criticism or an alternate view.* But its aims as Art really developed in the midst of industrial and socio-political revolution in Europe. French Revolution from 1789 to 1793, which brought down the rule of clergy and nobility, led to destruction of Bastille. These events propelled flourishing of this art form after the relaxation of press censorship. Ryan P. O'Donnell in his review of Michael Melot's "Caricature and the Revolution", observes that caricature has far reaching role of deconstructing "the political hierarchy polemically by means of an aesthetic medium for means of dissemination by a mass audience. As a destructive and reconstructive medium, the caricature serves as an ideal form as an instigator of social change within a period of revolution". The Art was exported or spread to England and with great commitment Sir David Low truthfully carried forward innovations in this critical, glorious Art of Cartoonish in service of 'common man'.

Karl Marx, admirer of this Art, comments on repetition of History of 1789-93 in 1848-51 French Revolutionary events as tragedy and farce. He treats it as parody, Nephew (Louis Bonaparte) imitating the role of his Uncle when he says, "And the sam *e caricature occurs in the circumstances attending the second edition of the Eighteenth Brumaire!"*

Sigmund Freud's works on Dreams & Jokes further explores the psychic origins of this Art- caricature. The analogy between the techniques of jokes and the dream work, both "share the cognitive mechanisms of condensations, displacement and indirect representation' (Ryan P. O'Donnell). He reiterates Freudian definition of "the joke" which "contributes highly to the *caricature's function,* due to its strongly gestural and automatist qualities, the caricature communicates more immediately to audiences through a regressive function that *invokes unconscious associations.* It is a medium whose primary goal is dissemination by a large audience. French revolution made the epochal impact on Europe and the world and the aesthetical medium". It was quite natural that in Sir David Low's Cartoonish, Sigmund Freud discovered the same objectives and mechanisms of 'Joke Work'. Here we discover the radical heritage of Sir David Low's cartoonish in depth psychology!

Legacy of Sir David Low- who aroused sense of Humor and not Sense of Horror

It is surprising that such vast populous country like India, despite producing innumerable cartoonists claiming to have been inspired by Sir David Low, could not produce even a *single known Cartoonist* (exception R. K. Laxman?) who could claim inheritance of the revolutionary or democratic critical tradition which Sir David Low inherited from his predecessors. India's last Fifty years of History has been severely affected by legacy of cartoonists who have targeted Literature and culture, have whacked minority Community through cartoon campaigns. There are cartoonists who misrepresented and subverted Sir David Low's glorious critical Art. It is matter of great concern to day that when once again rightwing Fascist groups and parties are clamoring and surging ahead for seizure of political power in years to come. Are the political cartoonists in India attempting to understand Sir David Low message of protection of human values and his fight against socio-political 'prejudice'? Sir David Low's Cornel Blimp fought against worst prejudices, intolerance, regional-linguistic chauvinism, corruption of values, authoritarianism and bigotry. He understood *'prejudice' as the reified mechanism which facilitates* easy ascendance of Fascism.

When Lord Moseley led 'Black Shirts' instigated burning of anti-fascist Exhibition Sir David Low suggested to stage a counter demonstration. When he failed to make it happen he dared to take on Lord Rothermere, proprietor of Briton's biggest most popular NEWS Paper 'Daily Mail' who was approver and very active supporter of 'Black Shirts' the rapidly growing NAZI British counterpart. (View Cartoon number DL0790 on British Cartoon Archive). It is noteworthy that the cartoon criticism (reminded me of 'Muzzler') on 'Nanny' of *'Daily Black Shirts'* by making a *composite phrase to integrate identities of 'Daily Mail' and 'Black Shirts'*. The Cartoon embarrassed Beaverbrook (Sir David Low's Employer) since Rothermere had helped Beaverbrook finance his purchase of the 'Evening Standard'. The satirical wit on 'DAILY MAIL' was explicit and clear. "We need a man of Action such as they have in Germany and Italy ......". The cartoon casted disguised Rothermere, Nanny, pushing the Baby cart with baby Black Shirts. NANNY imitates the NAZI Salute of Hitler and Mussolini who are shown to be raising their right hand with typical Salute. Both are hiding in their other hand the paper showing enormously rising figures of unemployment and trade deficit, wage down, prices up and tax burden in backyards of Germany and Italy. Sir David Low did not launch critique of 'Hitler' abroad pretentiously *but stood up courageously against 'Hitler from within', from within Briton!*

Recently established '**Indian Institute of cartoonists**' aims to foster democracy, takes clues from the experiences of fascism in European History and claims inspirations from Sir David Low, Shankar Pillai and R.K. Laxman is a welcome sign. But having Vision and living up to it are matters of retention of the heritage of that 'Glorious Art' and practicing it in India are things apart. With upcoming dangers and rising tide of prejudice, the need of the hour is to obtain unflinching support from 'un prejudiced' viewers as the source of energy and resource in defense of freedom. Rather than making limited appeal only to "Philanthropists, Corporates, Bankers, Industrialists, Businessman and Media Magnates to open their hearts and purses to further this cause. Spread the word around" it is essential to closely observe Beaverbrook – Sir David low's relationship. As an admirer of Sir David Low, I can only provide word of caution, while gathering of these resources presence of 'Black Ships' are likely to be there to subvert the vision. Sir David Low was not any one's hireling and must be credited for devising most innovative, 'out of Box' methods to ensure preservation of freedom of the Artist and remain loyal to popular cause for which this Art exists.

What cartoon admirers now anxiously look forward is emergence of New Breed of 'glorious cartoonish-artist', like Robert Minor, Rollin Kirby and Sir David Low who could launch inexorable unfailing criticism with an aim to "weaken prejudice and provoke people to use their own brains"! David Low's 'progress of man' remains an unfailing valid criticism of events in India of 1935, 1948, 1968, 1993, 2002 and its validity will continue *till the 'animal-man' becomes 'human'.*

I recall the image from memory of a photographic News Paper image encapsulates a lonely, unclaimed, dead body lying in the pool of blood, with police van on the background on the emptied streets of Mumbai in the wake of 1992-93 post Babri Masjid demolition and ask whether any cartoonist in India has produced even a single carton which can match the ethos of this real unforgettable image? Answer is 'No'. Indian cartoonists have not significantly resented the butcheries, like the one drawn by. Sir David, 'Progress of Man 1935'. That is the reason why Christopher Andreae in 'The Christian Science Monitor / October 18, 1985 calls Sir David Low, 'The thinking man's cartoonist'. "Sir David Low aroused Britain's sense of humor, not horror" He must be confronting Sir David Low with those who depicted others as 'swines and snakes' in their prejudiced cartoon campaigns to evoke mass hysteria and neurosis, who saw their objective in blinding the viewers with prejudice and aroused sense of horror through ugly 'counter violence' against the innocents, against working poor to settle one's own ancestral accounts. These are the conflicting legacies of 'artists' who arouse ordinary man to surge forward and those who reversed the historical progress and pull the social order backward!

India has yet to produce innovative cartoonists who can launch this glorious unfailing criticisms through cartoon campaigns. If not cartoonists, India has produced excellent Satirists like Vijay Tendulkar who raised his head above cultural and political degradation in his outstanding plays like 'Ghashiram Kotwal', which portrays the rise of Ghashiram, the hatchet man, a psychopath, rising amidst the decaying Peshwai of seventeenth century Pune to highlight the socio historical origins of terror outfits! Indian Cartoonists will have to 'Call up' his courageous critical satire, the soul of cartoonish, for times to come.

ARTICLE III

SAVARKAR – A POETIC GENIUS OR A PHILOSOPHER OF RAGE?

Response to Ashok Malik's 'Savarkar the man who saw tomorrow'

I happened to read with curiosity Ashok Malik's article "Savarkar - The man who saw tomorrow". This was the occasion of 125 th birth anniversary of Savarkar, (5 th June 2008) and is an astute defense of Savarkarism and his legacy. He sees Savarkar as Indian Alexander Hamilton, the "American nationalist, the forgotten founding father whose legacy is shaping up of the current American statehood, its policies and strategies.

Reference period of his article is 1980's in which Indian polity moved 'irrevocably to the right'. The course of History dramatically changed during this decade. 'The demonized, marginalized 'political Hindu' during his life time now stood vindicated' and "Savarkarism is more accepted than ever before". From the date of assassination of Mahatma Gandhi, the 'Political Hindu' under new combative organizational outfits began asserting himself and continued through Babri demolition and Gujarat holocaust. The course of events that followed shaped the Indian state, its policies and strategies. Crowning point came with unveiling of Savarkar's statue in the Parliament Central Hall in 2003 recognizing his prominent place in History and marked political triumph over cultural and political liberalism.

From dormant and insignificant presence in 1920's the "Hindu resurgence" has now acquired status of a menacing force and forms cultural bulwark around Indian State. Ashok Malik is happy that now 'the Hindu', not as an ascetic but as combative warrior is shaping up the polity exactly as Savarkar foresaw it. What Ashok Malik conceals is the fact that with this triumph of Hindu engaged in hatred in streets has opened up ruthless avenues for capitalist expansion and provided it with new repressive biting teeth for ensuring its unbridled hegemony amidst crumbling of working class resistance and ruling liberalism.

Ashok Malik confronts and targets the Marxist historians and left liberals who have ended up by becoming Nehruvian fellow travelers and pensioners of Indian state structure. He accuses them for having suppressed, demonized and despised Savarkar in their writing of the text books and distorted history. He conveniently prefers to blink his eye towards clemency petitions Savarkar made to ensure his release and towards the political manifesto of an ideologue who rebelled against British but capitulated to the rulers under rigorous punishment, about the 'patriot' who could not summon the mental forces against 'those above' and instead ended up by redirecting them against 'Mlenchaas'. For him such criticisms can be relegated as 'prejudiced'. He and his fellow travelers have valued him for his founding intellectual tradition for Hindu Nationalism, his blazing patriotism, and most importantly, his poetry and literature.

Interestingly Ashok Malik ridicules Manishankar Aiyer for mocking up at the 10 years Savarkar spent in cellular jail but remain deeply silent on Savarkar's metamorphoses in the that 'tiny cell' of Andaman which turned him into 'Warrior Hindu' who ridiculed Gandhian Non Violence but eschewed any confrontation with imperial capital. I seek to search for an answer to question 'what was the process of his becoming 'Hindu Warrior' to articulate a coherent Fascist psychopathic ideology of hate'.

Savarkar's followers are so proud of and have always referred him as 'Maha Kavi' (Greatest Poet). Unfortunately this remains an area in which Savarkar's political critiques have not ventured to probe. I intend to discover the 'birth' of his 'warrior psychology' by attempting to interpret his poetic creations in the 'tiny cell' of his Andaman imprisonment and in specific his '**KAMALA**', which is considered as magnum opus, to uncover the motive forces which constituted the **psychical** and mental foundations of his philosophy of hatred. KAMALA is a poetic narrative drama centered on its star character 'Kamala'. Final verses lead the readers in to dramatic episodes of brutal and barbaric splitting up of the pair of lovelom engrossed in intense romance (orgasm) and which left the charming phantasised female in dire state of anguish and insurmountable pain. Her unfulfilled erotic desires are sacrificed by male characters to perform heroic deeds of aggression against Muslims to avenge the defeat at Panipat.

Depth psychology has already substantiated that the poets create their world of phantasy and play to express the 'pleasure or distress' once they experienced in childhood, to master unsatisfying reality. Poet is compelled by the **'necessity'** to tell others and public at large what he suffers from or what gives him happiness and pleasure. This necessity in V.D. Savarkar's life is none other than the prison's unbearable conditions and struggle to articulate what he suffered from and conceal what he compromised with authorities. As victim of nervous illness, poets are obliged to tell their phantasies to release the repressed energies and derive enjoyments. We know that the motive forces of phantasies are the 'unfulfilled repressed wishes', which are mostly erotic in character. It is universally accepted that there is always and invariably, a 'woman' or 'lady' for whom heroic deeds are performed by the creators of phantasies. But the identity of the 'lady' is concealed in the phantasy due to reasons, may be, the poet is ashamed of it's 'direct expression' and being **culturally 'impermissible' hence the 'desired lady appears in distorted forms.** Whatever is repressed and in the state of unconscious, poets reveal it under conditions of relaxation of mental and physiological repression.

Under the spell of such conditions of relaxation of repression, the repressed wishes are allowed to come to the 'surface' in devious form. Any work of interpretation must try rescuing these 'desires' from their concealment and repression, in a way what pathology does it. Let us now travel through Savarkar's poetic creations in Andaman Jail.

Poetic Transition – Submerged in to world of phantasy.

Savarkar's poetic exploits can sharply be differentiated as those before and after his arrest and deportation to Andaman. The poems till 1908 represent the anguish and anger experienced by Brahmin castes after loosing political power and glory in Panipat battle. These compositions (ballads) articulate his youthful assertions to avenge the defeats. None of the poems give any indication (excluding stray poems on anguish of widows etc.) of social awareness about impact the British imperialism on classical Indian social- caste structure and changes ushered by modern capitalism. His revolt was propelled and fired by the social myths he inherited. In contrast to this, his poetic ventures in jail over a time span are characteristics of **complete despair and mental regression.**

Andaman poetry is remarkably 'inward looking', or can be described as protracted articulations of 'inner world' of 'phantasies' and 'dreams', **which he had become so fond of,** as noted by several **introductions** to his poems (Vol.7- Complete works of Savarkar).

There is an evolutionary pattern in these compositions and from period 1910 to 1920. Every subsequent poem has roots in the previous one or is further unfolding of the previous one. The 'epic' Kamala integrates all imageries, allusions, concepts, elements, themes and concerns expressed in earlier poetic compositions.

Interestingly number of poems revolves around definite constellation of characters. The four main characters, Mukul, Mukund, Premala and Mukund repeat over and over again in number of poems exhibiting his obsession with characters probably drawn from his earliest childhood family life.

There is a continuous regression, from his youthful fantasies, into the childhood or infancy, leading to complete **loss of reality** and **identification of reality with his dream life.** His outer world was burning with rage for avenging the defeats of Peshwas and Marathas in battle of Panipat at the hands of Mlenchaas.

We observe a pathological, obsessive compulsion on him to plunge into abyss and the world of his own 'dreams' (there are numerous references to dreams and observations on dreams in all his poetic compositions) and like Abhimanyu (son of Arjuna- the archer from Mahabharata) he had the means to pierce into the dark abyss but had *no means, inspiration and courage* at his disposal to 'progressively' come out of it. His **a-historical** journey invariably ends up at the discovery of a 'romantic lady' whose burning unfulfilled erotic desires lured him. This leads him finally to his creation, Kamala' drenched in romance and enveloped by rage and reprisal. The Hero of 'Kamala' is compelled to sacrifices her 'desires' to avenge the 'defeat of Panipat battles.

His poems are studded by erotic metaphors and imageries like 'Garden of Flowers, 'sacrifice of flowers' and the revengeful energies are however provided by the myths which had become part of his psychic life in the form of symbols. The principal characters of all these compositions exhibit influence of Indian and Greek Mythology. They are egocentric and all of them represent 'revenge' and blind rage.

Kamala has roots in number of previous compositions and merges with subsequent compositions. It has evolved over years. The Compositions like, "Chandoba, Chandoba (Hey moon), 'Sayanghanta' (Tolling of Evening Bells), 'Nidre' ('O' Sleep'), 'Kamala' and 'Virah shwasotshwas', have been reviewed as they form continuity and stages of escalation of his flowering fantasies. *The centre stage however is occupied by the phantasy named Kamala*. At the end I have attempted to demonstrate how **Kamala** was triggered by 'guilt of *patricide' rooted in another myth 'Krauch Vadh (Killing of male crane)* and 'flowered and supplemented by Vinayak's obsession with myth of Gajendra Moksha'** (deliverance of King Elephant God). These phantasies can be interpreted like dreams. We know well that 'Interpretation of dreams' is the royal road to penetrate through the 'primary psychic repressions' and know what goes on in the depths of the 'unconscious'. Now let me begin with few well-documented remarks, comments and criticisms on his compositions by well known Marathi critiques and News Paper Editorials of his time to reach to the core of his poetic thrust. (Refer Volume 7, Savarkar's Samagra Sahitya).

Remarks, reviews & criticisms.

'Maharashtra' DT. 26.08.1934 regards him as one of the finest poet in Human History. His metaphors, allusions, analogies, imagination and creativity are comparable to that of Sanskrit poet Kalidas's poetical creations. *His Epic Poem 'Kamala' will be remembered forever for its Form, aesthetic values and its dynamics.*

Kesari DT. 18.09.1934 comments that 'Kamala' the epic makes us to feel that Kalidas is reborn. Romance is 'Kamala's life and has been developed with supreme skills. **Dainik Kaal DT. 10.11.1950** compares Savarkar with Shakespeare.

Dr. P.N. Joshi (Vivek) dt. 29.05.1955. Comments that, 'Kamala' is the phantasied lady and is Savarkar's creation. Epic has it's origin in defeat of Maratha Kingdom at Panipat's war. This romantic creation by Savarkar however infringes on the boundaries of erotic and into the ridiculous (sexualized) zone of life. It is so powerful in its patriotic appeal that the 'Veer Ras' (**emotive aesthetics** of valor) appears to **stand and dance on the Head of the erotic'.** As if the 'Veer Ras' is expression of the erotic or sexual. This slightly critical comment shows some insights into the inner structure of this poetic creation and in a way admits that sexuality and eroticism as it's the foundation *on which has been built the superstructure of rage.*

Vedant Acharya Balashastri Hardas identifies KAMALA as "self narration of experiences in Savarkar's revolutionary life"

Almost each of the critiques have regarded 'Kamala' at the center of Savarkar's poetic creations.

Prof. V.G. Maydeo' introduction to this epic is lengthy. It introduces the events and sequence, which led to the creation of this Epic. The Epic with 882 verses was published in 1921, however it was composed much earlier, years before, in face of insurmountable hardships of the prison conditions where writing material was prohibited and attracted severe punishments if writing material was discovered in prison. As a solution to surmount this difficulty Savarkar used his already developed habit of reciting –remembering, learning his verses by heart for months and years together.

The detailed introduction to this composition, by Prof. V.G. Maydeo, make significant points about Epic 'Kamala'." It shows the influence of Milton's 'Paradize Lost' and Homer's 'ILIAD and ODYSSEY". This also is compounded by the influence of ancient 'poet of Erotic' Kalidas and myth of Krauncha Vadh (the Curse of Valmiki to Nishad), the hunter. ("Oh hunter you have killed the lovelom male of the Krauncha pair and left over the female in dire unbearable anguish, may you be starved of erotic pleasure throughout your life"). It is clear that Prof. Maydeo did encounter in 'Kamala' conglomeration and superimposition of symbols of 'Kirat Arjun War', 'Krauncha Vadh' of Valmiki and 'Oedipus' and other Greek Tragedies.

He also attributes this significant influence to father Damodarpant's teachings and guidance imparted to son Vinayak in his childhood. Prof. Maydeo dwells upon Vinayak's complete obsession with the defeat at Panipat battle which proved to be fatal for Maratha Kingdom under Peshwas. Above criticisms provided me with definite insights into structure and subject of the compositions and I suspect they may provide me the path for discovery of the 'psychological core' of 'Warrior Hindu'.

Trapped in the Dream Web

Savarkar's habit of weaving his dream phantasies began as a response or reaction to the protracted efforts to overcome and suppress his experienced instinctual, psychic and physical frustration of prison life. Historic accounts available reveal that it began immediately, within few months, from his deportation to Andaman Prison. It is highlighted by the Introduction to the poem, 'O' sleep. Savarkar's day began at 5 a.m. - chopping trees with a heavy wooden mallet and then he would be yoked to 'KOLU' (hand driven oil mill) each day and after completing the grueling punishment he **used to surrender himself to dreams, his favorite 'play'**. Savarkar became a **prolific dreamer** and, which enabled him to recall every day from his memories 'the beloved ones'. In fact the introduction says that **for a long time** after waking bells rang in morning hours at Andaman prison, *he failed to differentiate between* *his dreaming life and waking life,* indicating that **he was prisoner of his own dream images and dream events.** In his composition, 'Nidre' (O Sleep) and 'Sayanghanta' (Evening Bells when the prisoners were blocked in their cells), confirms that he was habituated to take shelters into dreaming. "The chariots of Dreams drive my 'self' to any destination on earth, in water, in air or in sky desired and facilitated my engagements and enjoyments" *with "beloved from my past life" and even the "new ones". (Verses 110 to 126).*

In poem 'O' sleep there is a further revelation of this process. In his passage into dream life and the cinematic image sequences, he identifies his penetration strategy (chakravyuh) with that of 'Abhimanyu', *who knew (learnt in his mother's womb) how to penetrate, but never knew how to come out!* "The chariot of time in dream life, drove my 'self' into the 'past', re-experience it. The Golden dreams enables even the 'old' (like 'Yayati') to make 'love' with 'charming' 'Rati', and enter into 'Love Union' with the 'beloved' of their childhood. The first kisses by the charming lady are re-experienced as 'the sexual pleasures'. Like lightning flash, the 'past' emerges as 'present' in this 'cinematic images' of dreams" (Verses 40 to 56). Overtly sexual imagery is repressed here to give way to regressive 'womb imagery'.

We encounter one more layer of the Dream Web in his poem, "Maranonmukh Shayyevar" (On a sick Bed – that threatened to be A Death Bed – Addressed to His sister in law). Vinita expressed his fears very loudly as he suspected having fallen victim to deadly Tuberculosis and was counting his last days. During his stroll outside prison cell on -a patch of green lawns - he was obsessed with the fears that "I could not induce myself to take further step since I fear my step may 'kill' the blooming seeds (Blades) of the grass" and was also obsessed with grave doubts about "my hand holding the morsel midway between the dish and mouth would automatically refuse to carry it further and from the very depth of my being a protest would arise, 'Hold'!" Since it will amount to be a criminal 'aborting' or murdering a child, and every child in the womb before its birth. Here he discusses at length 'rebirth' of flowers and seeds. He had a deep fear that he has become 'lunatic' (Verses 111 to 142). The entire journey of his poetic creations clearly reveals that he *was obsessed **with fear of dyeing 'childless'**.* This fear finds a crucial place in Kamala (verses 535-36 and other verses). In one of his mini poems, 'Departure from my dear Village' (Paragavi Jatana), he discloses the arrangement of his characters in 'Kamala'. In this poem he introduces the reader to Character named 'Premala'. In KAMALA and other compositions such as 'Virahoshwasotshwas', character 'Premala' makes her appearance as fiancée of central character 'Mukul'.

KAMALA has four principle characters with triangular romantic relationship, 'Kamala' the charming woman, Mukund (her Husband) and Mukul his dearest friend. This character Mukund (the name of youthful Lord Krishna) and 'Mukul' are pictured as two dearest and close friends (like blood brothers). Mukul's destiny in Kamala and the subsequent poetic composition 'Virahoshwasotshwas' (1915) with his heroic battles with the 'mlenchhas'- non Hindus (enemies of Chhatrapati Shivaji), his arrest and subsequent rigorous life imprisonment imposed in tiny cell (Kalkothadi). Vinayak Damodar Savarkar completely discloses his identity with the character 'Mukul' in the next poem, 'Virah Shwasoshwas' (sigh in anguish of separation). The Mukul, the central character of the poem is cursed by sage Valmiki and had to leave this world and abandon all pleasures of marital life. He is caught by enemy and jailed in 'Kalkothadi' (Dark Prison hole). This identification will put us firmly on the right tract of identification of all other characters in 'KAMALA'. Also, 'Mukul' means, 'Bud" or 'New Born' child, Mukund and Mukul probably are the elder brother, **'Babarao-Vinayak'or Father-Son' duo.** Mukund identifies **Mukul as his 'mirror image' like father treats his son hence I suspect that poet has created this character (Mukund) in the image of his father.**

Presence of large number of ambiguous terms, metaphors, allegories and symbols representing both, sexual and 'a-sexual' meanings provided Savarkar an opportunity to exert an erotic thrust in the entire composition. Like symbolic Abhimanyu he could enter in to the DREAM WEB of his primal desires for satisfaction of lusts but became its prisoner forever and lost his way to regain conscious existence!

Kamala –Vinayak's Personal Plot.

Overwhelming influence of Oedipal Greek Tragedies and the mythological story of 'Krauncha Vadh' is of uppermost interest in

Kamala. The tragic effects of the **conflict between the supreme power exercised by the Curse of sage Valmiki and the attempts by the principal characters of the tragedy to escape from the disastrous impact of the** curse by taking recourse to invasion on enemy camp of 'Mlenchaas' at the cost of imposing **supreme sacrifice** on **Kamala for the cause of the Hindu Rashtra. Poet used the myth of 'Gajendra Mokshya' to redeem from the curse of 'Krauncha (crane) Vadh'. This conflict forms the central driving motive force of 'KAMALA'.**

The story of Imaginary charming woman 'Kamala' unfolds in the phantasised 'Garden of flowers'. Garden is filled with heavenly attractions, erotic beauty and happiness. Kamala strolls in the Garden for offering prayers to the god with traditional grace and enters into erotic relationship with every object in the Garden. Mukund, her husband is hypnotized by her charms.

Almost 275 verses are dedicated to depict Kamala's tender relationships with various objects and behavior with her 'Mother in law'. She is married to Mukund at **very early age** of childhood (say five or six years of her age). The age factor gives an impression that Kamala's imaginary character and **images resembles some one Vinayak was closely related to, memory traces of his early age of his infancy and childhood (may be his mother! Vinayak lost his mother when he was nine)** Incidentally there are numerous references to dreams and metaphors in verses devoted to Mukund – Kamala romance, which corroborates that 'Kamala' is the woman of his dreams. Surprisingly, in composition 'Kamala' it is '**Mukul'** and not Mukund emerges as the principle and central character.

The sequence of events adopted in the verses resembles those in dreams, a rapid inexorable regression into childhood. They begin unfolding from the present to the deeper regions of the past, from youth to childhood, regression to infancy. *Father- Son- Mother Relations suddenly acquire the center stage of this phantasy 'Kamala'.* The entry of character Mukul, Mukund's dearest friend is intriguing. Mukul's gestures and behavior towards Kamala resembles that of mother –child but at the same time, have equally affectionate-romantic overtones. On more than one occasion **Mukund sees Mukul as his own mirror image** and painfully addresses his preparedness to relinquish marital enjoyments and **abstain from sexual** pleasures as a gesture of deep emotional bond he shares with Mukul and to demonstrate his solidarity with Mukuls' commitment as fierce warrior and to take on enemies of Shivaji and avenge defeat of Bhausaheb Peshwa at Panipat.

Mukund and Mukul's are engaged in lengthy dialogues full of jests and poking fun of each other, revolve around Kamala, her unsatisfied emotional and erotic desires. Mukul rigorously impresses upon Mukund to first attend to Kalama's marital desires and the importance of procreation and son's commitment (in Hindu Religion) in discharging his duty to procreate and fulfill father's desires before father's death. (Verses 506 to 545). These dialogs are significant in one more way. The poem incorporates the fears expounded earlier in poem, 'Maranonmukhshyayya' above. The *inhibiting fears of impotency or dieing 'childless'* had gripped Vinayak. Here we have a confirmation that Mukund – Mukul' are the characters created by the poet, Vinayak himself, by splitting his own ego to perform different roles. We get confirmation of our enquiry so far **in Prof. V.G. Maydeo's identification of KAMALA as 'poetic narration in which poet exercises his right to conceal and articulate his ideas under ruse**.

Rapid transition of this poetics into drama makes it clear that V. D. Savarkar has created these two and other characters to satisfy some compulsive logic of his own burning sexual desires and concealing of Oedipal desires and the experienced guilt. It is an extremely 'Egocentric Phantasy' in which the principle characters are the result of splitting up of the ego of the poet into more than one 'part egos'. *Poet sits 'inside' the second character (Mukul) and observes and intervenes in the unfolding course of events and shapes them*. On the other hand the main character (Mukund) stands aloof and plays insignificant role in unfolding drama. 'Mukul' (bud) takes charge of **the *heroic deeds* w**hile Mukund plays the role of second fiddle. Through the introduction of these characters V.D. Savarkar has **personified** the conflicting currents of his own mental life.

(Kraunch Vadh-Patricide or Fatricide?)

It is strange that Mukul articulates incredible 'insights' into grasping Kamala's burning desires. In fact he is shown as a character making innumerable attempts to 'induce' through jests 'Mukund to enter into 'love act- orgasm' with Kamala to ensure procreation. This persistency of perusal to highlight need to procreate and Mukul's deep insights into Kamala's longings and Mukund's **'inability to act in crucial matter', his hesitations and inhibitions** confirms that through this conflict Vinayak as a *poet, has articulated his 'self doubts' and repressed fears of dieing childless*.

Mukul- Mukund conversations have many twists and turns. They are intended to create intense erotic atmosphere and are prelude to anxious and dramatic events *unfolding at accelerated pace*. In several verses Mukul questions Mukund's intentions to abstain from erotic life till Mukul gets married. It compels Mukul to express his *profound guilt* and is forced to ask Mukund *"Am I (my mind) so savage and monstrous to wish scorching of Kamala's erotic desires before their blossoming into flower. (Verses 533-36)*.

The conflict between affectionate gestures towards Mukund and unconscious desire to disengage Mukund at the peak moment of 'orgasm' forms the psychological settings and framework determining the course of rapid unfolding of dramatic events. Mukul is shown to be bearing the guilt and mental burden of Sage Valmiki's curse to hunter Nishad. The events which are cramped into next hundred verses provide the evidence of Mukul's desperate attempt to absolve himself from curse.

Vinayak navigates through the 'darkest erotic imagery' to impress upon significance of relishing erotic moments and 'sowing the seeds' in intense act of love and procreation. He emphasizes that these moments alone have created Hindu warrior saviors 'born in epochs' like Vikramaditya, Gurugobindsingh and Chatrapati Shivaji who trounced the invading Muslim Rulers. He illustrates importance of erotic life of Hindu Gods and goddesses from Hindu scriptures to authenticate his arguments (verses 791 to 805). From here he takes the readers down on to dream scene of 'parental union'. Vinayak has mustered all his energies and capacities to create the desired erotic imagery to reach up to imagined scene of 'love Act' of Kamala – Mukund. He has likened it with the **'love act of parents'** – 'Kamasan' (orgiastic postures of parents). He pictures it as the moment of total hypnosis where the couple is engrossed (like cranes- Kraunch birds!). All critics excluding Dr. P.N. Joshi have kept deafening silence on these verses. Dr. P. N. Joshi ((**Vivek**) **dt. 29.05.1955**) has termed these as as 'highly erotic and infringing upon the boundaries of ridiculous or vulgar"! The poet here **discloses his own** repressed scoptophilic 'phantasy'. The phantasy passes on to next strange scene which confirms his *Oedipal guilt of wishing breakage of parental engagement.*

At this peak moment of the 'phantasized orgasm', uncanny episode breaks out. Frightening noises and galloping sounds of horses emerging from the unknown source cleaves the dream scene. We enter into new scenario. Tense Mukul wearing soldier's uniform steps down from the saddle of the horse and knocks doors of the 'Mukund –Kamala's Royal Bedroom ('shayyagrah') to read out the King's Order. Mukul now addresses Mukund. "I am in a hurry. I must leave for final battle with the enemies 'Mlenchaas' (Muslims) to attack enemy camp. Shri Bhau (who was deadly wounded in Panipat battle and finally perished at Kurukshetra), has ordered me to take revenge of killings of Maratha warriors like Dattaji and now my 'shiledars' (sergeants) are waiting for my orders to invade the enemy camps! As a Maratha warrior what should I be asking for is a blessings from mother (presumably Kamala?) But dear Mukund, please do not join me. Kamala must be fast asleep and I must avoid making you a request to leave Kamala. It will amount to throwing her into fire, sacrificing her life.

Mukul troubled by the curse, takes over the role of Achilles the primal character in THE ILIAD, the fierce Greek warrior who is driven by rage, pride and honor. On the other hand his dearest brother-friend (Mukund) is duty bound by Rules of Religion to procreate and fulfill Kamala's desires. Hence to absolve himself from the curse, Mukul prepares himself for going into the final battle field all alone to take revenge of defeat at Panipat (At the hands of Ahmed Shah Abdali). He wows to fight like the warriors of Shivaji to defend HINDUTWA!

Does he escape impact of the Oedipal guilt or escape from Valmiki's curse? Mukund suddenly decides to disobey Mukul's advices and follows Mukul on to the battle field. Disengagement of the Kraunch pair is complete. KAMALA is wounded and is in insurmountable grief and has horrendous dream! **Here we find integration and superimposition of two distinct moments in the drama, one tragic and other barbaric irrational. The escape route for Mukul, for avoiding punishment for fratricide, lies in fleeing from spheres of sexuality into spheres of battlefield and genocidal politics of violence.** Mukul replaces patricide by fratricide in thoughts; unconscious urge for revenge is thus complete! The unconscious sexual energies are marshaled for aggressive and violent ends. Poet's personal plot wears the garbs of 'Krounch vadh', as anxiety reaction to his own inhibitions and fears of dyeing childless and wishing an escape from the curse for achieving **immortality and redemption.**

From Fratricide to Genocide -Redemption from curse

The 'Oedipal' dream fantasy of forcible raking up of the parental union and sage Valmiki's curse to 'Hindu' responsible for splitting the orgasm of 'loved ones' hangs heavily on Mukul. 'Virahshwasoshwas' (composition subsequent to KAMALA) echoes this guilt and self pity for Andaman Imprisonment (Kalkothadi) as punishment earned for a crime committed and accumulated over hundred births till rebirth in human life. Panicked by the eventuality of the curse, Poet had struggled in KAMALA for redemption and immortality. The way to absolve lies in his barbaric choice of sacrificing Kamala to respond to Shivaji's call for aggression on Mlenchaas. Critics are **struck by grafting of myth of Gajendra Moksha' on his guilt of Krauncha Vadh in KAMALA. Mukul decides to go all alone** on to the battle field. But alas, the inevitable aught to happen. Final events end up in raking up the Kamala- Mukund union and leaving Kamala in insurmountable grief and anguish. The mystical and unthinkable happenings are forced by 'Mukul's sudden re-entry on to the scene, 'Mukund –Kamala's 'shayyagrah' (Royal Bedroom).

The final verses exhibit 'uncanny characteristics' like those in horror dreams in which familiar becomes unfamiliar and threatening. It final verses are marked by the external stimuli disturbing the continuation of dream (ringing of prison bells at dawn), produces the images of sound of galloping horses emerging from unknown source which inevitably rakes up 'Mukund – Kamala' union.

In subsequent scene (following scene of parental orgiastic posture) Mukund refuses to oblige Mukul and argues, "My dear Mukul, I can only disregard your advice when enemies of Hindutwa have surrounded us, when old and young are dieing. Can I avoid responding to Shivaji's call? Are not myself and you (Mukul) same and identical, undifferentiated? Kamala is asleep on the Royal Bed and I salute her, bow before her in anguish, 'O', God save Kamala! (Verses 865 to 874). The chariots of Horses begin galloping towards the camps of 'mlenchhas'(Muslims). The Mukund – Kamala separation is achieved. 'Kraunch vadha' is complete, female Crunch is in dire state of pain and anguish. *Kamala wakes up with dreadful anxiety dream* scenes of aggression on enemy camps of Mlenchaas and in which loving beds are set on fire. The condensation and superimposition of dream imagery is revealed in the ending verses quoted bellow.

"Horses Yell and Gallop forward, Breathless Soldiers march ahead, Enemy camp is under attack, Guns roar endlessly, swords cross and shine, Roars Every where, Loving Beds (Kamala's) turn into Battlefields. **Dream turns into truth!**"

Royal Bed lamp flares up, wild fire spreads and engulf, Colors of love (erotic desires) turn Bloody Red, and Garden of Flowers is set on fire. 'O' my Blossoming Bakula (Flowers), your fragrance is in vain, ('O' Kamala) your cries are in vain and your beloved disappear The Royal Beds are set on fire and **Dreams turn into truth!** (Verses 871 to 882)

Most horrendous and stunning end of the composition KAMALA compels the readers to hear the cries and yells of 'Kamala', *who dreamt of lighting up of royal beds in with fire.* The war mongers fail her; sacrifice her for their own 'immortality' and redemption and to avenge the defeat at Panipat battlefield! Kamala and 'Mlenchas' (Muslims) both are sacrificed!

Mukul / Vinayak takes hold of the fallen saffron Hindu flag of slain Maratha Peshwas, Sadashivraobhau and Vishwasrao *from Panipat battle field and in real life unfurls it as National flag of Hindu India.* It symbolically represents the rage and combative revenge to integrate and camouflage violence with ascetic tradition. Genocide replaces fratricide. Oedipal desires are transformed into violence against 'Muslims'. Genocide becomes the way out in reality for escaping from guilt, a permanent flowering phantasy. In *final verses Savarkar adumbrated his mature political theory that the escape root for resolution of Oedipal conflict lies in elevation of dream phantasy life on to political horizon and displacement of instinctual forces on to 'Other', as hatred of Muslims and violent genocide!*

Poet aims at instigating the readers and audience by evoking valor (Rudra Ras) and battle cry of warriors and bids to hypnotize readers with patriotism. However in the process he discloses the process of escalation of rage and violence driven by repressed instinctual forces. From the burning bed of Kamala emerge the triumph of the Psychopaths and psychotics in the battle field. Symbols of erotic are camouflaged by blood symbols. Garden of flowers is set on fire! Kamala sacrifices her life for liberation of 'Vinayak! Dreams come true! Reality submerges and Virtual dream reality emerges- that of 'Hindu Rashtra'.

In Interpretation of final episode we come across compounding of images from 'preconscious' and 'unconscious'. We suspect that sounds of galloping horses disturbing the 'Kamala –Mukund union' are likely to be caused by external stimulus, the disturbing ringing sounds of 'wake up bells' **in Andaman prison in morning hours**. However the dream wish to continue the sleep masters these external stimuli and fulfills the wish of continuation of and prolonged dreaming. *The conversation leading to aggression on camp of mlenchaas to avenge the defeat seems to be provided by the desires residing in 'preconscious' while the Oedipal dream phantasy of splitting the pair, 'love act of parents' is triggered by psycho sexual force residing in the 'unconscious'.*

Through the interpretation of Kamala I have tried to discover various layers of Vinayak's psychic reality, in which a variant of 'Oedipal Complex', guilt of the Krauncha Vadh, forms the bottom most layer of impulse. Composition *'KAMALA can be seen as response or reaction to Vinayak's one or series of Oedipal dreams in Andaman jail.* Troubled by the curse, Vinayak attempts to absolve himself by taking flight to battlefield against Muslims by leaving the popular masses languishing under plague of repression, economic, social and cultural exploitation and slavery of imperial capital.

Comparison of Savarkar's KAMALA by few commentators with Shakespeare (who also deals with subject of relations of son to his parents *or subject of childlessness)* or with Oedipus of Sophocles is ridiculous in terms of treatment of the subject. Oedipus when felt troubled by recollection of oracle of the sage, unravels the patricidal and lustful past with 'ever-mounting excitation' with sole purpose of repealing the plague ravaging Thebes. In doing so poet compels the readers and audience to recognize their own minds and discover the same suppressed impulses. If *"Oedipus Rex,* expresses the consciousness of a whole people", KAMALA is uncanny horror dream- phantasy propelled by sexual fury unleashed by Mukul, is articulated as *political violence for pulling down the dams of civilization which can manifest itself only as Fascism*!

Mukul's revolt in 'Kamala' leads to a horrendous end! When 'dreams turn into truth', Mukul –Mukund now merge into each other and emerge as psychopath waging war against Muslims. *In my interpretation I have done nothing other turning upside down and contextualized the mildest criticism leveled by Dr. P. N. Joshi (Vivek). 'Veer Ras' appears to stand on the Head of the erotic' to uncover the birth of violence unleashed by 'Warrior Hindu'.*

Savarkar's 'Kamala' does not give any message of confrontation to those 'above', a threat which would have alarmed British imperial capital. Instead he chose to exhume his sexual past to take revenge and fulfill his political obligations to Sadashivrao Bhau and Vishwasrao peshwa who were killed by Ibrahim Lodhi's army in panipat battle. (Incidentally on birth of his son in 1928, Savarkar named d his son 'Vishwas') Here is a poet whose courage had already crumbled to pieces in the initial period of Andaman, even in thought, and so also in poetic creations, could not have been expected to take on the mighty imperial capital. Instead he plunged into darkness and lacked courage to pursue the truth and opted for desperate attempt to unleash violence in the arena of political culture for personal redemption. Hence it shatters the claim as great piece of Literature and Art!

Founding of the Fascist Philosophy

I have sketched an analysis of psychic events and mental- character structure of Savarkar's ideology of rage against Muslim and other communities through interpretation of his poetic phantasy ventures in Andaman. *His Andaman poetry provides us the window to view and witness how the upper most surface layers of his psychic life,* the revengeful blood symbols and sacrificial imagery, is completely subsumed and enslaved by erotic instincts seething down in to in unconscious.

I wish to turn to another element of final episodes leading to hysterical identifications of 'Warrior Hindus'. Mukund abandoning Kamala and joining Mukul for final battle with Muslims and conversation, "Are not myself and you (Mukul) same and identical, undifferentiated?" fulfills another condition of 'dream phantasy'. It conceals Mukul's fratricidal hostility towards Mukund. In doing so Vinayak discloses the process of 'hysterical identification' in formation of 'fascist group' by way of condensation of two figures on the *foundations of seething sexual instincts*. This process of distortion is possibly brought about by psychological 'censorship' exercised by resistance to disclosure of Oedipal desires! We know from psychoanalysis that Identification is 'highly important factor in the mechanism of symptoms' which are part of dream work. We can now conclude that V.D. Savarkar has expounded his philosophical theory of fascism organized Fascist groups now we can proceed to examine few of his political and communal responses in literature and latter life.

When transferred to Ratnangiri Prison V.D. Savarkar's 'mental reality' was formed, reified and crystallized. Poetics of Andaman continued to impact his waking life in Ratnangiri Jail. His 'Purification Movement', launched in Jail did not spare a single opportunity to propagate hate campaign against Muslim prisoners and to demolish their 'arrogance'. "I resorted to my tried out medicine! I caught hold of, organized couple of professional 'expert Hindu dacoits .... The bunch of criminals included an old criminal who was given harshest punishments at least a few times". V. D. Savarkar personally instigated organized **'anti Muslim' bash** in Ratnangiri and Yerawada Prisons. Detailed account of it appears in 'Majhi Janmathep' (pages 503 to 505). The issues such as

'Religious Purification' and opposition to 'Dalit exclusion' and planned exclusion of 'Mlenchaas- Christians' and 'social reforms for casteless Hindu Nation' became main plank for launching fetish for resurrection of 'Casteless and classless Hindu nation State'.

In a sub chapter '**Ultimate Suicidal attacks**' of 'Mazi Janmathep' Savarkar mentions about series of suicidal compulsive attacks he underwent (1921-23). We have already uncovered Savarkar's psychic breakdowns as the basis of his ideology and the driving force of his philosophy. In 1923 his Book- "Hindutwa- who is Hindu" outlined the cornerstones of his Hindu Nationalism and Hindu Nation State, which come close to those of *Rassenideologie* of Nazis in Germany and which denied citizenship to Muslims and Christians. The man who saw Hindutwa as an Indian 'Risorgimento' finally became the fundamental ideologue of the worst bloodsheds in the Indian history with Hindu Muslim confrontations. *Yes and true, Ashok Malik's statement Savarkarism 'has never been more alive" is proved in the facts of genocides and holocausts.*

Marzia Casolari's research paper refers to 21 st session of Hind Mahasabha in 1939 when Savarkar made one of the most explicit comparisons between the Muslim question in India and the Jewish problem in Germany. But research paper does not throw any surprise at us. Interpretation of Savarkar's poetic venture KAMALA disclose his triad before and till 1938 to support Hitler's anti-Jewish policy of extermination of Jews and articulation of veiled threats of identical fate for Muslims in India. This article can be just a foot note if Marxists and P sychoanalysts can plunge into the debate at this critical hour.

'My Legacy'- Undisguised Barbarism

I have tried to deduce from the conflict or the two concurrent or mutually opposing views of those who regard him as Hindu nationalist *par excellence, an archetype, 'warrior ideal' who spent his imprisoned years in horrific conditions, alone in a 'tiny cell' and opposed views of the liberals like Manishankar Aiyer who treat him as villain for whom* he was a 'villain' in view of surrender to British Imperialism by making clemency petitions and giving undertakings.

But both ignored, suppress or unaware of *how horrific the dream is and being the deranged vision* which can work only as a fetish for providing barbaric form to capitalist rule and provide sanctions for holocausts. Amidst the retreat of the Nehruvianism, Ashok Malik greets with pleasure the rapid speedy ascendance of the fascist organizations, their might and their influence in shaping the Indian state. The signs of merging and confluence of two seemingly antithetical trends, Warrior and ascetic. One "RSS working from the bottom up from grass root communities" and two Savarkarism providing lethal philosophical leadership for the organized 'Warrior Hindu Groups' committed to extermination and holocaust fully supplement each other.

His claim that the triumph of 'political Hindu', of a polity sensitive to the "Hindu cultural mainstay of Indian Nationhood", "while eschewing ritualism and dogma, incorporating robust Nationalism" also sounds hollow and pathetic. What we see today's 'political Hindu' participating in Gujarat or Mumbai genocides is mass of petty bourgeoisie and lumpen in despair completely submerged in to ritualism, phantasies and dogma whose psychical foundation remain the mythological symbols expressing the guilt residing in their psyche. His concealed claim that Savarkar was 'rationalist' is equally misplaced. His concealed claim that Savarkar was 'rationStructure of KAMALA provides us enough evidence of the irrational deranged mental make up. Unlike Oedipus, who "resolved the dark enigma", who "recognized the guilt in his own mind" and who perused his quest till the guilt is brought to light, Savarkar had no courage and commitment to do any thing of the sort. Instead he attempted to escape from his 'individual fate' and for achieving 'Redemption. **Philosophy of Oedipus is quest for truth. Vinayak's philosophy is obsesses ion with immortality and redemption.** Hence he takes plunge into archaic darkness and guides his 'fellow travelers' to direct the seething instincts against 'Mlenchaas'.

Today's scenario differs from that of V.D. Savarkar's time (as prisoner in 1924) by **degrees** only but on sprawling magnitude and scale. Gujarat's carnage instigated and protected in year 2002 witnessed the **replay of** tiny event of riot in Ratnagiri and Yerawada Prisons in 1921-23. Today mass of psychotic groups from the ranks of petty bourgeoisie in despair are led by ideologues of lesser caliber such as Togadias and Bajarang Dal activists driven by identical phantasies, dreams and guilt. They are inching forward violently and silently to influence and infiltrate political state and its powerful institutions. Today it is time to *closely* understand 'Savarkarism' and phantasies of lesser gods more seriously. If Savarkar understood 'statecraft and the importance of state power', the mantle of historical task in unveiling and bursting the fetish of "Casteless and classless Hindu resurgent state"' falls on shoulders of mass of working people, industrial workforce, the tribal, the landless rural poor, leaders of Indian labor, trade unions and class of intellectuals committed to pursuance of truth and to close the ranks and take on ghosts of Savarkar more seriously and not to dismiss their programs as blend of reaction and dreams.

After the crushing of the working class revolution in Germany and Europe after end of First World War and murdering of its leadership like Rosa Luxemburg and Karl Liebnetcht, German labor committed this historic mistake and their organizations got shattered and opened avenues for barbaric holocaust under third Reich striving for destruction of humanity. It is time to say 'Never Again', 'Never Again' to the *deranged vision- 'Legacy of resurrection of Fascist Hindu State'*.

ARTICLE IV

POLITICAL PSYCHOLOGY OF ANNAJEES

"Hegel remarks somewhere that all great world-historic facts and personages appear, so to speak, twice. He forgot to add: the first time as tragedy, the second time as farce." As historian, Karl Marx in preface to Second edition of "Eighteenth Brumaire" says that he intended to "demonstrate how the class struggle in France, created circumstances and relationships that made it possible for a grotesque mediocrity to play a hero's part".

Political fantasy and Revolutions of 2011

The year 2011 saw re-birth of Mahatma Gandhi when agitation led by 'Ex- Army man- Anna Hazare' became euphoric and spilled over into Delhi's Ramleela ground and across the metropolitan cities and urban areas. Modern day Mahatma Gandhi led the 'India against corruption' movement with sole fanatic aim of implementation of 'Strong Lokpal', was propelled by despair and anguish of the middle classes. It rattled the centrally ruled congress government. Release from Tihar Jail, turned Anna into a National leader and a hero. The first year of the decade had ushered politicization of under-privileged classes which had lost capacity to strike back against impact of rising tide of neo liberal globalization which in last three decades has re-casted the entire class structure and relations in India. TV Channels hailed the agitation and the yearnings for immediate implementation of 'Strong Lokpal' as

India's second freedom struggle. Media followed and covered Annajee for 24x7 and projected the aging hero as New Father of the nation, national hero and Modern Mahatma Gandhi. "We have not seen Gandhi but we have participated with modern Gandhi's struggle for freedom against corruption." middle classes reacted.

The profound financial scams of extremely high magnitude, exploding one after another so to say, displayed the bankruptcy of the ruling class of politicians. Shrill, grating and ear piercing propaganda led and hyped by TV NEWS Channels and Media cleverly concealed from the public gaze the reckless manipulations and awesome corrupt practices and influences exercised by financial and industrial tycoons. It camouflaged competing interests of internationally ambitious capital and neo liberalism on the political executive and on Annajee's movement itself! The central cabinet and Prime minister exhibited their shear helplessness in dealing with the retrograde movement which had only one and sole frightening weapon at their disposal, the threat of 'Indefinite Fast', equivalent of suicide bombing to compel implementation of 'Strong Jan Lokpal Bill'.

It all began fuming out in March 2011 when Anna Hazare announced his Indefinite or Fast unto Death fight against corruption and was amplified on much larger scale in June 2011. The frustration and anxieties of crowds exploded on political horizon. Politically, the most backward and immature sections of the nation, middle classes, the trading community and petit Bourgeoisie took upon themselves the role of 'savior of the nation' and unleashed movement for "National Renaissance and redemption" amidst 'the national disaster and shame' perpetuated by sprawling and spiraling corruption. 'Save India' from corruption enshrined and embodied in lower rungs of bureaucracy and ruling political class became the slogan of the day. TV NEWS media played the role of a vanguard in projecting an all encompassing *fetish of corruption* to facilitate political fusion of these classes into oneness under Annajee's 'Anti Corruption' umbrella. Corruption was equated with covert disease contaminating and ruining the vital functions of the nation.

Just before scams broke out, the corporate Media, MNCs and Industrial captions who *were promised peace on labor front* after the G20 world summit and after drubbing the left and winning the confidence vote in Parliament, were singing chorus in one voice, *"Singh is King" for PM who was the first to ushered the reforms in 1991.* On sensing the magnitude of discontent spilling over of an urban resistance movement with street demonstrations and led by aged authoritarian leader with parochial and highly mediocre background, government officials and Ministerial trio began appeasing Annajee. The unconquerable Anna, became the, custodian and signifier of 'anti corruption' obsession and fanatical irrational fury of middle classes. Truly a pathologic character occupied the political stage for months together. Threatening Indian Political establishment with near suicidal weapon of 'indefinite fast' was unusual and new. Raked up ghosts of Scams forced PM and the trio to bend down on their knees before Annajee to douse the fire and to prevent total erosion of middle class support.

TV News agencies promoting hysteria and 'I am Anna' cult were engaged in drawing parallels between Annaji's Ramlila Ground procession and revolutionary upsurge in Egypt and victorious celebrations in Tahrir Square and across Egypt. Annajee's demand of 'watchdog institute of 'strong lokpal', focused on 'employees of lower bureaucracy' and total exclusion of corporate, when confronted with those of Egyptian upsurge exposes Annajee's 'anti corruption' episode as grotesque fantasy! While summing up of the major popular economic demands of Egyptian revolution, Mostafa Omar, the American –Egyptian writer activist in his **"Egypt's unfinished revolution"** sums up the demands surfacing with the call for ouster of Mubarak and the corrupt regime run by his henchmen. "Workers' demands vary from one sector to another, but they revolve around four main issues: Workers everywhere want to raise wages and benefits; they want permanent status for the millions who have been working as temporary workers, sometimes on contracts as short as three months; they *want an end to the neo-liberal policies of privatization of companies, and many in the public sector are calling for the re-nationalization of companies that were privatized and sold to investors at below market values; and they want the ouster of all the corrupt CEOs appointed by Mubarak"*.

The contrasting set of economic and political demands exposes not only the class characters but also the *political psychology of Annaji movement*. In Indian context the contrast becomes magnified and sharper when compared with another coeval parallel movement occupying the same time span from March 2011 to November 2011 of equal magnitude and scale. The mass strike and agitations inspired by Maruti Suzuki workers. TV and Mass media camouflaged and pushed under the carpet the much more intense protest movement of the working masses involving much larger crowds. It paid attention to it only to the extent of covering vitriolic propaganda against production losses. Annaji's movement rode on to a furious fantasy of political turmoil while the fearless series of strikes and different forms of protests by Maruti Suzuki workers *provided panic jerks to the social foundations of Neo Liberalism.* The demands awakened the hopes of working classes and electrified segments of working masses across India and abroad. It was first display of a spontaneous united upheaval and solidarity action after the defeat of textile strike in Mumbai. This *forward* and *upward movement* exposed the industrial legal political system and perils of neo liberal corporate capitalism which had pushed working classes into state of oblivion.

Tall and Invincible Anna

If historical parallel is to be drawn it can be with impact of failed Panama Project of the 'French Panama Canal Company' in which Ferdinand and Charles de Lesseps were both indicted for fraud in 1889. The project led to loss of thousands of lives and millions of Francs. Political bribery of French Parliamentarians was laid bare and were accused of 'not representing the people' in moral sense! Corruption undermined rule of law and let loose irrational powers and mass anger. Anti-Semites, the enemies of 'Republic' broke through the soil and seething buried tensions of French Society gushed out. When France erupted into turmoil it also questioned the liberals in Austrian and German political systems as well. It raised serious doubts, 'what is the use of Parliament which is vulnerable to corruption and assaults'?

Cultural corruption advancing rapidly with neo liberal onslaught and 'downfall' of moral values provided Anna team a readily available cannon fodder to stir up the 'corruption complex' and patriotic fury which evoked sense of national redemption and cry for liberation of the motherland from the noose of the political and bueurocratic crooks.

Annajee signified the instinctual and psychopathologic rage. The reactionary and irrational content of his populist campaign disguised and concealed the class belongings. Arvind Kejriwal, Kiran Bedi and others created corporate scaffolding for him to make Anna stands 'tall' and invincible. During December 2011 flopped campaign Kiran Bedi tweeted for encouragement, "Corporate world in Mumbai now has an option of joining the movement. Support Anna, get the law and help shoot up Sensex" and exposed who calls the shots. Throughout the upswing of the movement Annajee remained under ideological siege of Arvind Kejriwal, Kiran Bedi, Manish Shishodia and others who represent the face of Neo liberalism and its CEO culture. The clique was incessantly engaged in concealing the enormity and extent of involvement of Corporate players in promoting culture of corruption in social life and within the ranks and files of political democracy. But a leader is nevertheless and is always a relation between people and the individual who embodies their collective demand. Anna has claimed that not only he knows the Gandhian language of non-violence but also Shivaji's language of sword. He intended to invoke popular compound image of and for himself as an aggressive adamant and ruthless furor wearing a Gandhi cap. Finally 2011 ended by turning the hero in to Gandhi's caricature! Anna's personality and his peculiar aggressive and dictatorial traits became sharper the more prominent as soon as he sought in *himself the secrets of his success in popular mobilization*. But that is exactly why *anatomy of his personality* explains why in this transitional time it was difficult to have another political figure in the same measure, ideologically bankrupt and completely unaware of the anonymous driving forces of history. Events on national scale cleared his way to become short term transitional patriarch and a hero destined to get exhausted.

Psychoanalytic Literature and political anatomy of 'Modern Gandhi'

Literature in abundant was published and posted on internet during 2011 dealing with Gandhi and the modern day Gandhi- Annajee. Unfortunately little has been done to bring out psychological foundations of their political anatomies and historical significance of the movements. I have reluctantly engaged myself to attempt and undertake the resolution of these conflicting interpretations made by two social activists.

"What clicks with Anna Hazare is his apparent simplicity, rooted ness in the familiar Hindu tradition and the penchant for *nationalist rhetoric.* The manner in which he has taken up the issue of corruption sans its complexity gels well with the large population of urban upper-caste middle class, which, variously, grudge the government not being conducive enough to their progress" (Dr.Anand Teltumbde).

G.R. Khairnar (Anti Corruption and demolition crusader) slams this comparison, "There is a huge difference, it's almost like the earth and the sky". Anna Hazare's abusive and sexualized language (Calling opponents 'Banjz- infertile- impotent woman) also came under his severe criticism.

Middle classes discovered in Anna the modern 'Mahatma Gandhi'. However the comparison ends with his dhoti and Gandhi cap he wears and his mimicry of Gandhi! It will be interesting to confront political psychology of Annajee and Political character logy of Gandhi. Anna has kept his personal life within moral limits defined by him the most importantly self imposed limits on instinctual urges and 'non corrupt', puritanism in particular. However his mystical and opaque personality cracks up as soon as he raises his finger in the style of a dictator abusing his opponents and calling them impotent. Violent sexualized imagery beneath Annajee's Gandhian language betrayed at an occasion when he hit out at his opponents, "banjh kya jaane prasuti vedana (what would an infertile woman know about labor pain). The remarks invited severest criticisms from Women Activists. Activists said "the remark was insensate and smacked of sexist mentality. (Lawyer and women rights activist Flavia Agnes)).

Annajee seems to be unaware that Gandhi is not known for using abusive or coarse language against women. Psychoanalyst Mr. Sudhir Kakker explored Gandhi's personality in his well known fiction "Mahatma and Mira" where in he weaves the facts with fiction in the story of Gandhiji's relationship with Madeleine Slade, in the mirror image of Lord Krishna and Mira. It depicts reciprocal relationship of devotion, affection and sexual restraints. Gandhi worked all along to exercise control over the 'sexual serpent' and its expressions, which springs and recoils even in dreams, to attain Brahmacharya (celibacy)! Gandhi's experiments with truth were aimed at becoming celibacy, identifying, inhibiting and controlling sexual urges which he believed, if not subjected to control, could lead to unleashing of social and political violence and rage.

Annajee remained ignorant and prisoner of seething, irrational powers of instinctual rage even though he remained unmarried and underwent total instinctual repression during early life and military tenure in particular, ending with war with Pakistan. Controlling the instinctual drives forms the basis of Gandhian non violence. M.K. Gandhi restrained the mass movements by not allowing (he believed so) the unconscious sexual fire to engulf the behavior of the masses in the street and turning of the sexual rage into violence against State. ***Anna did the opposite.*** He uses sexual imagery alluding to corruption metaphors to unleash fury of irrational instincts and generate anti- corruption hatred mania amongst middle classes. He claims that he could survive the 'indefinite fasting' because of his celibacy and possibly by keeping away from female body which contaminates morality and health. Celibacy seems to be the ultimate solution of all human problems. However for Annajee celibacy involves suppressing the sexual drives and processes, unlike Gandhi's attempt to establish 'sexual control'.

Psychoanalytical studies on ***psychopathic characters*** on stage and linguistics may prove decisive in this regard. Literary criticisms committed to interpretation of patriarchal social order which invariably refer to Shakespeare. Hamlet's (Prince of Denmark) comment on correlation of corruption and downfall of kingdom of Denmark is suggestive. Despite being so honest queen, Gertrude was affectionate towards her son Hamlet, however never confessed to any 'sin' before her death, which is interpreted as being naivety and leniency towards 'corruption' in Denmark. Incestuous marriage of (Hamlet's) mother Gertrude to her brother-in-law was for him illustration of corruption and 'contaminated female sexuality'. Hamlet's sexual disgust and deepening melancholy, bitterness and cynicism used to ***trigger his suicidal self-hatred.*** Helen Reakes student of Shakespeare says, "The fear of female sexuality coincides with Hamlet's belief that corruption and (sexual) contamination are primarily derivatives of female body. Hamlet repetitively associates the origin of sin to his birth, acting almost in Hamlet's fantasies as a reason for man's corruption. It shows how words *corruption and contaminated sexuality are treated as synonymous, identical or are united in unconscious. Linguistic unity between sexual contamination and corruption provides us insights into organic link between psychical processes of 'anti- corruption complex' and 'oedipal complex' and the power of the symbol to provoke irrational fury. It provides us the clues to understand how the prejudices in social unconscious are provoked as hatred.*

In the eyes of populace, the bursting of very high magnitude scams rolling out one after another not only created political circumstances which completely undermined the political claims of development, smashed national dignity, brought on to the surface mockery of legal system and rule of law but also made the representative parliamentary electoral system susceptible to onslaught of fury of irrational forces. Psychoanalytic literature and interpretations enables us to reach into the bottom most meaning of 'corruption' metaphors within the social unconscious. The political events leading to Annajee's arrest proved to be the most powerful instigating and provoking agent to inflame the psychical tensions embedded in the reified and ossified caste, religious and gender based prejudices of the traditional Indian social order. The collective prejudices compounded with genuine anger against corruption were let loose and began out pouring in the form of copious streams of resistance. It generated the pathologically obsessive *fantasy of all inclusive Anti Corruption Lokpal Bill.* Anna Team and the TV Media could bring about fusion of all middle class prejudices and system of metaphors, considered as National Heritage and rode on the agitation as patriots aiming for salvaging the National Pride'. Kiran Bedi waved the national Flags. Crowds sung the War songs and national Anthem as patriotism on display. The outcry for "strong Lokpal' circulated at rocketing speed. Sanjay Kumar (Aug 31, 2011, Countercurrents) covers the hatred involved in high peak of the agitation, during the Ramleela procession and the rally which followed metaphors of prejudices integrated the movement in August 2011. "It was obvious during the rally that a virulent, sexist, castiest and openly patriarchal fringe was trying to make its presence felt in the Anna gathering, which undoubtedly attained a mass character"

Suicidal Urges and Origins of 'Strong Lokpal'

Anna Hazare's nearly pathologic obsession with derogative usage of most contemptuous word (complete lack even of sympathy) 'Baanz' used in rural India, a stigma on childless woman, and which invites a social boycott fort her is indicative of his parochial intellectual stature! Parochial Annajee overnight discovered himself as mass leader of a nation whose credentials across the globe as 'nation on the move' crashed to debris as 'scams prone corrupt nation'. His 'indefinite fast' or suicidal threats became the appropriate but only formless expression of despair of the middle classes. In his rise as 'national hero' he was assisted by congress ministerial-office bearer trio who went for his character assassination which proved to be 'God' given help in the conjecture of events in bolstering his Gandhian 'puritanical' and 'corruption free' credentials and forcing government for virtual capitulation.

Annaji's character traits have another element – his punitive approach and his attitude to consider everything non- negotiable! From Ralegaon-sidhi, he brought in to the movement the barbaric traits of punitive culture compounded with authoritarian military methods. He has been projecting Ralegaonsidhi (which he had shaped after returning from Warfront), model dominated by rich peasants, as ideal economic, social and political model and as ideal prescription for Nation! The parochial Patriarch, he probably considers himself to be, as incarnation of figures of Swami Vivekananda (ideologue of Hindutva) and his ancestor Guru 'Yadav Baba' as his superego the formidable agent of repression. He succeeded in imposing his own moral code of social conduct and legal system as harbinger of 'punitive' system, like public parades, flogging in open, military fashioned court martial of culprits and defending 'death by hanging' for corrupts as national prescriptions. He had practiced by himself these barbaric & primitive punishments of flogging meted out to wrong doers and liquor consumers. His oratories in Delhi and his postures resembles style of *military dictators angry with pitfalls, shortfalls of democracies, inefficient working procedure and its ability to offer quick solutionsand hence ordering punitive decrees!*

Gandhiji mobilized the peasantry in ruins in the spate of advancing capitalism under colonial rule and made the mass subservient to growing clout of 'National Capitalists'. Anna performs different role, role of an arrogant fanatic, in crisis of neo-liberal representative democracy by offering most autocratic solution of 'Strong Lokpal Bill'.

Anna ignores all forms of atrocities and exploitations, communal- fascist violence, injustice meted out to dalits and women. and launched 'all exclusive' agitation to subsume the anger of the middle classes, to veil the briberies paid by Capitalists, CEOs and executives to gain licenses to exploit public funds and finances, natural wealth or other assets and instead direct it against small corruptions in lower bureaucracy.

We learn from Annajee that he had faced with severe suicidal urge during his youth but reading Vivekananda enabled him to overcome it. I may be that Anna may have been struggling against melancholic depression! Sigmund Freud and subsequently Melanie Klein have shown that severe depression arising out of loss of earlier psychic objects (love object) manifests itself in paranoia, anxieties or schizophrenia. Annajee suffers from severe depressions and could overcome it by re-strengthening the repression. ***Ironically, instinctual urges breaking through the surface of repression results into generation of insurmountable anxieties, in the form of suicidal urges. One suspect the weapon, 'Fast unto Death' threats as the effective weapon to scare the opponents is manifestation*** *of same urges! Anna's threats on 'strong Lokpal' may be viewed as his internal psychic need to repress the anxieties and build as 'self observing' superego*! In times of crisis situations, coercive 'Fast unto death', Self immolation' threats have always evoked and generated mass paranoia and anxieties, and can trigger mass movement of elite and middle classes.

In Anna's psyche, contaminated sexuality (immorality) and corruption are tightly and organically intertwined and Anna succeeded in unifying and welding these anxieties of the middle classes and transferred on to political horizon. Solution offered by him is nothing less than a step towards 'Regimentation of 'Indian Nation state'.

This is precisely the *pathologic genesis* of his proposed ultimate solution 'watch dog' Institutions, described by many as 'parallel oligarchy' or 'huge autocratic monster' to regulate the corruption and the 'instinctual contamination' Psychoanalyst will certainly see in it 'externalization' of *'psychical internal hatchet'* and projection of repressive psychic agency ruling the instinctual and impulsive life on to political expression of population. Strong 'Lokpal' agency is an articulation of Annajee's *image of his own psychic repressive agency and resultant of inner psychic conflict*. The rebellion of bound instincts obeys the laws of displacement and the anxiety generated is deflected on to political system. In this sense alone I appreciate Sukumar Muralidharan's comment, "Political corruption is a convenient target onto which this whole complex of anxieties could be shifted". It becomes Annajee's *'final solution'*. For him, in his psyche, all versions of democracies promote bribery. The outcome aimed at could be 'Military Rule' to reconstitute the crumbling Nation State, stifling the voices of descent from working masses and making the middle classes subservient to "Neo Liberalism", reincarnate the hegemony of *'National Capitalist Rule'*.

Conflicting Discourse of the decade- Egypt and India.

Political analyst, Sukumar Muralidharan assessed media responses to two movements, which will decide the discourse of the decade. Annajee & Maruti Suzuki which occupied the centre stage of economic-socio-political discourse says, "The Maruti Suzuki agitation and the Anna movement. "Clearly, the media had sanctified Hazare's movement, bestowed it with the legitimacy that the trade union agitation did not deserve".

Maruti Suzuki struggle stands in conflict with Anna movement. The long drawn out struggle, mini- mass strike and workers mobilization exhibited continuous forward thrust and passion for achieving freedom and inspiration to repeal the 'repressive control and governance of working conditions of production and life'. In this sense Maruti Suzuki workers followed the discourse set by Egypt. As a role model of *Neo liberal mode of production,* Maruti Suzuki has installed a totalitarian PMS System (Production Monitoring Supervisory' System, a watchdog institution) within shops with robotized production processes and across offices to subsume the 'labor productivity' down to details. Mass strike on the miniature scale reflects something similar to what conditions prevailed earlier in Egypt, Tunisia, and Arab World. The striving for mass democracy, a collective upward thrust, drive to form independent Trade Unions, spontaneous urge to occupy work places, demonstrations and formations of steering committees signals a new era. Maruti case study posted on web says, "In many ways, the 13-day strike at Maruti Suzuki India Ltd, India's largest automobile manufacturer, was a wake-up call for the Indian corporate sector. Not only did it illustrate the unity among the company's workers, but with workers and unions across states voicing support, it threatened to flare up into a wider industrial dispute, giving *strong signals of a resurgence of trade union activity in the country*".

Egypt's Tahrir Square 'witnessed historical moments of ouster of Autocratic Rule of Hosni Mubarak and repeal of proxy rule of Military Junta! Mustafa Omar reports, "Participants of Egypt upheavals were millions of workers, poor peasants, poor housewives from Cairo, Suez and Alexandria, and overthrew the regime of the "rich and the businessmen who think they could run the country as if it was their own private company" (Mustafa Omar). The revolution changed the social Institutions of oppression and rediscovered themselves"! He further states, "The masses of poor and working-class people who took part in the uprising--as everyone else who took part--wanted democratic reforms. But workers and the poor also want social justice and the redistribution of the country's wealth after 30 years of privatization, impoverishment and neo-liberal policies pushed by the Mubarak regime. *They struggled for the "Economic Democracy". Revolutionary workers 'locked' corrupt CEOs or stop the "disrespectful treatment at work, temporary contracts, and terrible health care provisions and on and on".*

Weren't these demands central to Maruti Suzuki struggle? Wasn't corruption the integral part of Hosni Mubarak's led Neo Liberal regime? Weren't scams of 2G scale part of Egyptian neo liberal regime? Then why the working masses of Egypt did not advocate and demand similar to "Strong Lokpal" solution?

The Indian capitalist class and the embedded corporate world are probably much stronger and integrated into the world capitalism than the Egyptian ruling class. Hence has used all its ideological and repressive powers to put an end to Maruti Suzuki struggle and pursue to push Annajee's political agenda of 'strong lokpal or could find an escape root of shifting the investments to safe heavens of labor peace in Gujarat?. In preceding years, series of strikes in Automobile Industry ranging from Ford, Marimalai Nagar, near Chennai, GM, Halol, Gujarat, Mahindra at Nasik, Hyundai at Chennai and other strikes in have laid the foundations of maturation of thoroughgoing revolutionary changes in Capital- labor relationship in India and globally! Today's seemingly non- political industrial agitations and solidarity collective actions is a slow process of weaving and knitting of the working classes. The new generation of workers, educated, skilled are learning to understand the causes of their hardships and subservience to conditions of work. Recently Cyrus P. Mistry visited Gandhinagar to pursue the interests of Tata Power Ltd and NANO plant. Whether Maurti Suzuki also flees to heavens and heart land of 'labor peace' in Gujarat or Thailand or Germany the specter of working class movement may haunt it across! For Indian subcontinent and globally social economic and political *discourse of this decade or probably of this Century* has already been set! **The struggles in Gurgaon or in Chennai have signaled to the millions and millions of wage earners, contract laborers, and informal laborers about ways to advance their struggle on to global arena.**

In an unrelated event, on December 7, 2011, a rudimentary meeting of representatives of Tata Steel workers' unions from different countries, including Australia, India, Great Britain, New Zealand and North America, took place in Jakarta under the banner of Tata Steel Network. Eighty One thousand factory workers across continents sought to join hands in solidarity through a 'transnational employee union'. Sudharshan Rao Sarde, at International Metal Workers Federation meeting said, "It is like how Karl Marx envisaged: workers of the world unite," Despite the metaphoric value of the event, it can be seen as high point indicating that aspirations of working classes are providing upward push for globalization as *against the rightward, regressive movement of the capital.*

The panic within the ranks of corporate world can be judged by Suzuki's decision to migrate its expansion plans to Gujarat. After TATA the automobile giant began rallying behind BJP to facilitate the industrial development.

The well established hegemonic arrogance of capitalism which restructured the industrial social relations for last three decades, after defeats of Mumbai Textile workers and demise of textile industry in Gujarat, has been literally pierced by Maruti Strike alone. Globally it brought in to open the underlying *changing perceptions and reciprocal relationships of three classes,* working class, Middle class and the capitalist class and their *upward, regressive and rightward movements.* The movements represent new political discourse of conflict of working class thrust *for globalization* verses obsessive 'Strong Lokpal' agitation led by *a pathological character on the political stage* to reinstall the confidence and hegemony of the *'National capitalist'* ?

Annajee team targeted the 'Political corruption' and worked hard to transfer the complex of psycho- instinctual anxieties of the middle and lower middle classes to unleash the fury. The fanatical stress on urgently creating a watchdog and authoritarian, "efficient, superior and strong" Lokpal Institution also amounted to indiscriminate casting aspersions on the day today life of nearly three crores of working population! It boils down to inflicting and imposing on national scale a repressive 'self observing' mental agency and repressing of all socio-economic aspirations of working masses by creating frightening ghost and fetish of 'anti- corruption'. Only a fanatic with militarist bent of mind can advocate suppression of basic freedom and human rights, can project single *objective 'patriotic' program for 'redemption of Indian Nation', ask for militarist regimentation within population,* with anxiety ridden foul cry to 'save India' from contamination of morality and leave neo liberalism to go amok! By asserting the colossal failure of representative democracy and ignorant of driving forces of history Annajee became devils advocate of totalitarian Military rule amidst the scream of 'disintegration of nation state'. Despite seeming decline of Annajee's movement, it has laid bare the receptivity for a 'self observing psychological totalitarian agency' within mental framework of mass of middle classes and the mass psychology for an invitation to Military dictatorship in times to come. *The irrational movement of Lokpal, worked exactly in opposition to the spirit of Egyptian revolution,* its forward, globalizing and upward push, which tirelessly works for overthrow of henchman of neo liberalism Hosni Mmubarak and Military Junta, both.

Anil Pundlik Gokhale, is an Engineer by profession and has been a reader and student of Marxist and Freudian literature for last four decades. He has been a professional translator of medical and other literature from English to Marathi. As a non regular writer on politicalliterature he has always been attempting to integrate Psychology and Marxism. He is the author of 'Condensation And Condescension In Dreams And History: Essay - From Sigmund Freud To E P Thompson' by Author House London.

www.ingramcontent.com/pod-product-compliance
Lightning Source LLC
Chambersburg PA
CBHW050426290526
45786CB00003B/1407